START-A-CRAFT

Julie Crosby
May 95
(Brighton)

START-A-CRAFT

Basketmaking

Get started in a new craft with easy-to-follow projects for beginners

POLLY POLLOCK

NEW BURLINGTON BOOKS

A QUINTET BOOK

Published by New Burlington Books
6 Blundell Street
London N7 9BH

ISBN 1-85348-626-4

This book was designed and produced by
Quintet Publishing Limited
6 Blundell Street
London N7 9BH

Creative Director: Richard Dewing
Designer: Ian Hunt
Project Editor: Stefanie Foster
Copy Editor: Michelle Clark
Illustrator: Jeremy Siddall
Photographer: Ian Howes

Typeset in Great Britain by
Central Southern Typesetters, Eastbourne
Manufactured in Hong Kong by
Regent Publishing Services Limited
Printed in China
Leefung-Asco Printers Limited

DEDICATION

Granwin, Granpa and MM

Contents

Introduction

Basketry is an ancient craft, probably predating even pottery and textiles, which has a history going back many thousands of years.

Very early baskets were likely to have been crude throwaway containers – like early shopping bags, perhaps – made on the spot as the need arose, to hold and transport gathered food, for example. Such baskets are still made today. In parts of Southeast Asia, for example, you may still be given a roughly woven palm-leaf basket instead of a plastic bag in which to carry your shopping home. This type of basket is made from whatever is easily available and is suited to weaving quickly into the required form.

Basketry has evolved over the centuries as a response to this need to protect and contain things, from eggs to trash. The specific forms reflect the wide-ranging yet particular uses that it has served – traps to catch fish and lobsters, baskets and mats used when preparing or serving food, baskets to transport racing pigeons, hats to protect their wearers from the sun and rain, even simple houses, and last, but not least, baskets for carrying all sorts of things in. If you visit a museum with an ethnographic section, you are likely to see some of the surprising and varied functions that basketry fulfils.

In addition to being an ancient craft, basketry is an almost universal one; many of its forms and techniques have evolved independently in different parts of the world. The different techniques used to make baskets largely reflect the materials available to the makers. Although there are many variations within basketry techniques, they can be grouped into five main categories:

- ◊ wicker
- ◊ plaiting
- ◊ coiling
- ◊ twining
- ◊ knotting and netting

This book introduces the first three.

WICKER

This technique is used with rigid materials such as willow, bamboo and round reed, which is used for four projects in this book.

Round reed is the stem of the climbing palm generally known as rattan, imported mainly from Southeast Asia. By the time it reaches the user, it has gone through several processes to produce long strands tied in 1 pound hanks or coils. One of these steps involves milling it to produce the different thicknesses, categorized according to the diameter of the strand and measured in millimeters. The size categories range from very, very fine (No. 00, which is 1.5mm in diameter) to middle range (No. 3½, which is 2.5mm, and No. 4, which is 2.65mm), right up to handle reed (No. 10, which is 8mm in diameter). The size used will depend, first, on the planned size and function of the basket and, second, the position and function of the reed in the basket, so, for example, base sticks are thicker than side spokes.

Processed round reed has a neutral, creamy color, which can be rather dull and lifeless, although there are weaves that produce interesting textures. However, as round reed takes some dyes very easily, all sorts of possibilities for color and pattern are there to be explored.

PLAITING

Plaiting uses materials that are naturally (or can be made into) long, flat, ribbon-like strips, such as palm leaves or birch bark.

Basketmakers have always used whatever materials they could find easily and which could be used for weaving. In modern, urban environments, one material available to the ecologically minded basketmaker is discarded cardboard boxes. Painted and cut up into long strips, they are an ideal material for plaited baskets – and they are free!

COILING

While there are some similarities between the wicker and plaiting techniques, the technique of coiling is unique. Even though the techniques are different, the materials used are often the same or similar. For instance, lengths of split palm leaves can be used for stitching around a core bundle of straw or grass. Some materials are used for both stitching and core material, such as raffia, which comes from the leaves of the raffia palm.

HOW TO USE THIS BOOK

This book is divided into three sections, distinguished from each other by the materials and techniques used.

In each section, the first project is the most straight-forward and introduces basic techniques. Subsequent projects introduce additional techniques as well as consolidating the skills already learned. For example, in order to weave the Cylindrical Basket on page 19, it is helpful to have made several bases and to have practiced the weaves, which are introduced in the Placemat and Tablemat projects that precede it. So, if you are a beginner, you can expect better results if you build on your skills progressively rather than starting straight away, say, with the Shopping Basket on page 23.

Before starting any of the projects, read the introduction to that section; it gives important information about techniques you will need to know when working on each basket. When a technique is introduced in the step-by-step instructions, it will appear in italics, i.e., now *make the slath*. This indicates that you should refer to that technique at the beginning of the chapter.

It is also very useful to read the instructions for the project all the way through before starting so you have an overall picture in your mind of what you are doing and how this relates to the other steps and the appearance of the finished basket.

Regarding tools and equipment, no great investment is required as you do not need many items and the ones you do need are "low-tech." Indeed, you may well have all the necessary things already; for example, scissors, string, clothespins. For those items you do not have immediate access to, it is usually possible to improvise until you are able to buy or borrow the tools mentioned. For example, you could use a skewer, an awl or a bodkin.

A NOTE FOR LEFT-HANDED BASKETMAKERS

All the projects are described with a right-handed person in mind, that is, working from left to right. It is much easier for a left-handed person to work right to left and there is no reason why this can't be done, but for reasons of space it wasn't possible to include reverse instructions in this book.

FINAL NOTE

I hope that you enjoy making these projects and, equally important, that you enjoy using them, too.

CHAPTER 1

USING ROUND REED

INTRODUCTION

The sizes of round reed used for the four projects in this section are:

- ◊ handle reed (8 or 10mm)
- ◊ No. 5½ or 6 (4–4.5mm)
- ◊ No. 5 (3.5mm)
- ◊ No. 4 (2.75mm)
- ◊ No. 3½ (2.5mm)

If you cannot find the exact sizes specified for a particular project, one size up or down from that given will almost certainly work just as well. For example, the difference between No. 3½ (2.5mm) and No. 7 (2.75mm) cane is negligible – 0.25mm, or a tiny fraction of an inch.

THE TECHNIQUES YOU NEED TO KNOW TO MAKE THE PROJECTS

Several techniques are common to the projects that follow, and these are explained below. In the projects, the techniques used are listed under the materials and references to them in the step-by-step instructions are printed in *italics* where they first occur. Until you are familiar with the various techniques, it is best to read through the relevant sections below before starting a project, as there are all sorts of tips and clear explanations to help you achieve the best results. These are not described in such detail in the projects.

PREPARING ROUND REED FOR USE

Round reed should always be worked when it is wet because, in its dry state, it is quite brittle. However, too much soaking can discolor it badly, so, whenever possible, use hot water for soaking. If you have to use cold water, you will need to soak the round reed for a bit longer.

As a rough guide, the thicker sizes need to soak for a maximum of about 5 to 10 minutes in hot water. The thinner the round reed, the less soaking time it will need. Try to get used to how long to soak the various sizes by feel. It is ready to use when you can bend it to a 90° angle without it breaking. However, some reeds will always crack a little, no matter what you do to soften them.

To keep the round reed damp while the project is in progress, use a shower or plant sprayer in preference to soaking it again.

Remember *never* to leave round reed to dry in an airless place, such as in a plastic bag, as it will become moldy in a surprisingly short space of time.

Cutting cane

Get into the habit of cutting round reed on a slant. With few exceptions, it is very useful to have a point at the end of a piece of round reed; it is easier to insert it into previous weaving or thread through gaps as required.

Dyeing round reed

In its natural state, round reed is a creamy-white color. Round reed takes dye very well, and it is interesting to experiment with the color patterns different weaves produce. An added advantage is that you can make something to fit in with the color scheme of a particular room.

It does not take long to dye round reed, but it is very important that the safety precautions detailed in the dyeing instructions are followed exactly and that you work in a well-ventilated room.

You can either use the dyed round reed immediately or leave it in a dry, airy place to dry out. Note that you should never leave damp round reed in a plastic bag as it will become moldy.

You will need

- ◊ Face mask
- ◊ Rubber gloves
- ◊ Old metal pan or bucket (not to be re-used for holding food as toxic traces can remain)
- ◊ Suitable dye (enough to dye about 1lb of cane)
- ◊ Mordant—some salt for hot-water dyes, but read the manufacturer's instructions
- ◊ Pan and water
- ◊ Stick
- ◊ Newspaper

1 Wind 2 or 3 strands of round reed into a bundle and do the same with the rest of the round reed. Don't make the bundles too tight or you will get a tie-dyed effect. Soak the bundles in hot water for about 5 minutes.

1

2

3

4

2 Prepare the dye solution. Put on the face mask and rubber gloves, then, in the pan or bucket, mix together the dye, the mordant, and water according to the manufacturer's instructions. Stir well with a stick.

3 Put the soaked bundles of round reed into the dye. To make sure that the round reed is dyed evenly, don't put too many bundles in at once, and keep it moving.

4 When the round reed is a good strong color, rinse it well under cold running water.

WEAVING A ROUND BASE

Making the slath

The number of sticks used will vary from project to project – the instructions that follow give an example of making slath for a round-based basket, using the "wicker" technique.

1
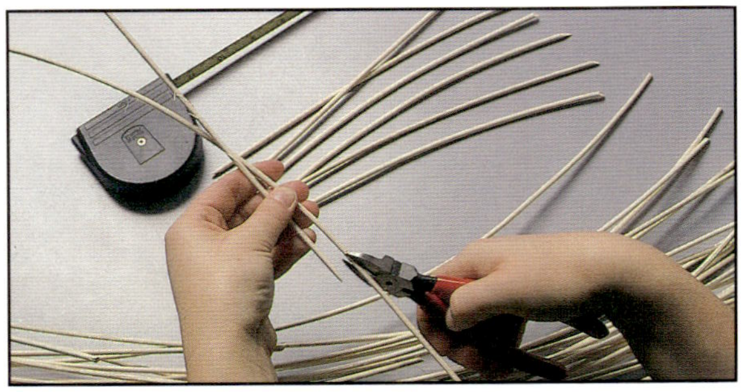

1 Cut 8 sticks to the length required for the diameter of the base plus 1½–2inches.

2
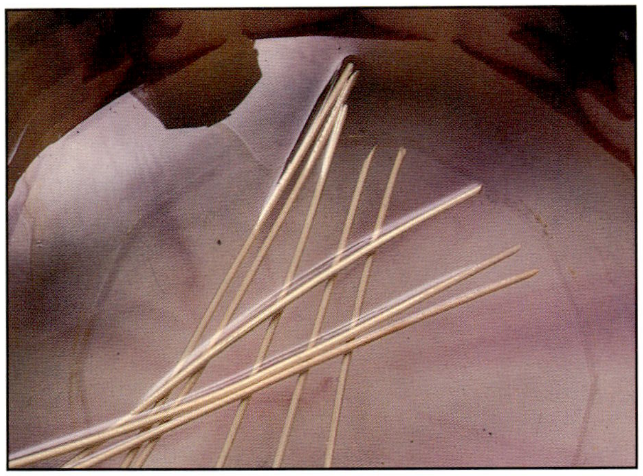

2 Soak the sticks in warm to hot water for 5 to 10 minutes to soften them.

3

3 Pierce the center of 1 stick using a bodkin and push it along the bodkin. Repeat this process with 3 more sticks so that you have 4 sticks on the bodkin.

4

4 Without removing the bodkin, thread 1 of the remaining sticks through the pierced sticks. Then, remove the bodkin and thread the remaining 3 sticks through the hole.

Tying in the slath

1

1 Take a length of soaked round reed, bend it at the center, and loop it around 1 arm of the slath (see above). This is the first stage of "tying in the slath" and looks neatest when the loop of weaving round reed lies parallel to the pierced sticks.

2

2 Holding the slath in your left hand, hold the weaving reed so that you have a right-hand and left-hand strand. These strands are called "weavers." Hold down the right-hand weaver with your left thumb and, working clockwise, take the left-hand weaver across the top arm of the slath, down behind the second arm, then up, finishing at the front. Give the slath a quarter turn counterclockwise.

3

3 Repeat step 2, keeping the weaving as tight and neat as possible. Work 3 rows in this way. Now the process of "tying in the slath" is complete. The weave used for tying in the slath and for the rest of the base is "twining".

4

5

6

Continuing the base

4 The arms of the slath are now opened up into pairs. Do this by firmly pulling the sticks apart after working the last stroke of row 3 and bringing the weaver up to the front between the pairs of stakes.

5 Continue twining, opening out the sticks until you have 8 evenly spaced pairs. Work 2 rows.

6 Then, continuing twining, open out all the sticks to singles. To keep the weaving tight and neat, as you take the left-hand weaver down and behind, pull down on the weaver. Take care to maintain this tension as you bring the weaver back to the front.

WEAVES

TWINING

1 If you begin twining after a block of waling (for the sides of the Cylindrical Basket, for example) lay 2 weavers – **a** and **b** – into 2 consecutive spaces, between spokes **1** and **2**, and **2** and **3**.

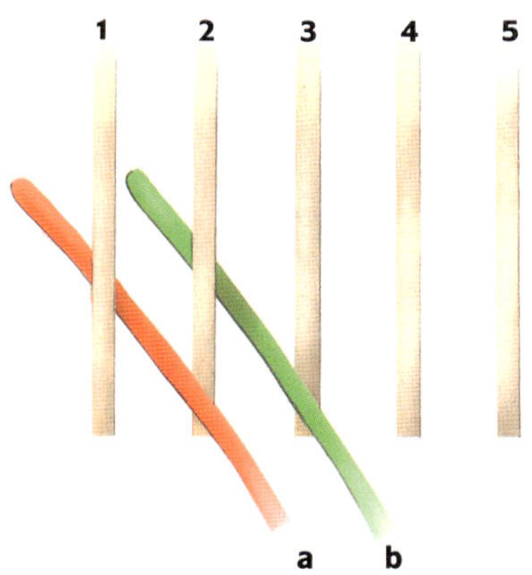

2 Take strand **a**, which is the left-hand weaver, in front of spoke **2**, over the top of strand **b**, behind spoke **3**, to lie between spokes **3** and **4**. Then take strand **b** – which is now the left-hand weaver – in front of spoke **3**, over the top of strand **a**, behind spoke **4**, to lie between spokes **4** and **5**. Continue like this, always taking the left-hand weaver in front of one spoke and then behind one spoke. So **a** will travel in front of **6** and behind **7**, and so on.

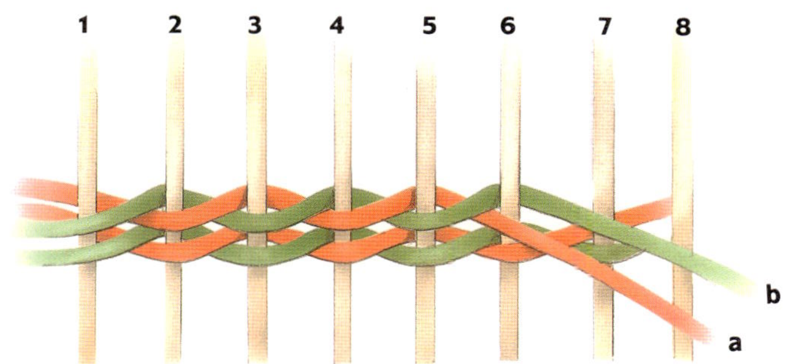

Adding a new weaver

1 When one of the existing weavers begins to run out – when there is about 2inches left – you will need to join in a new weaver (in twining, the weaver you are joining must always be the left-hand one). Join in the new weaver – **c** – as shown. Note that the new weaver is inserted toward the left of the space between stakes **1** and **2**, and goes under both the existing weavers **a** and **b**.

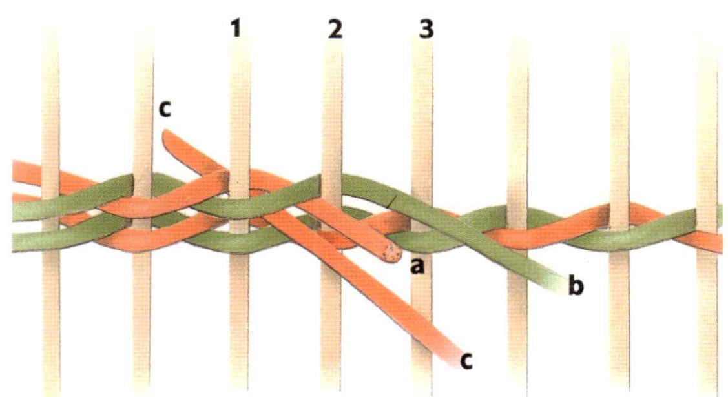

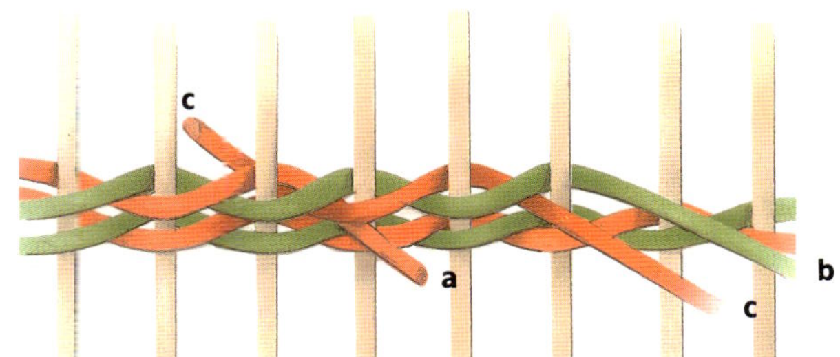

2 Pick up the new weaver – **c** – and continue twining. Work it over the old end in front of spoke **2** and behind spoke **3**.

Completing the twining

On the last stroke of the final round of twining, as you bring the left-hand weaver back to the front, thread it under the top strand of the row below to secure it. The other weaver is automatically trapped during this process.

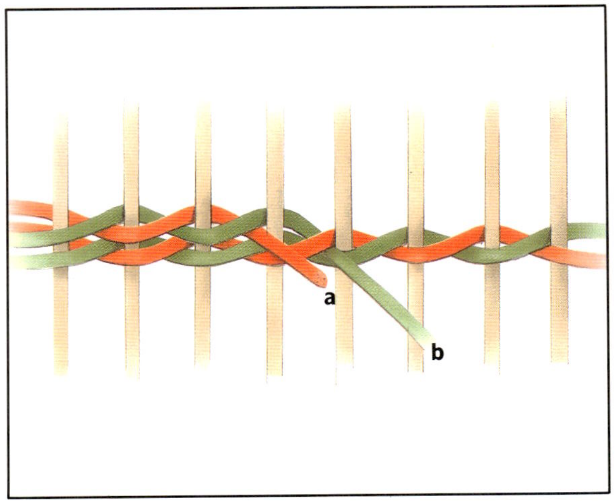

THREE-ROD WALE

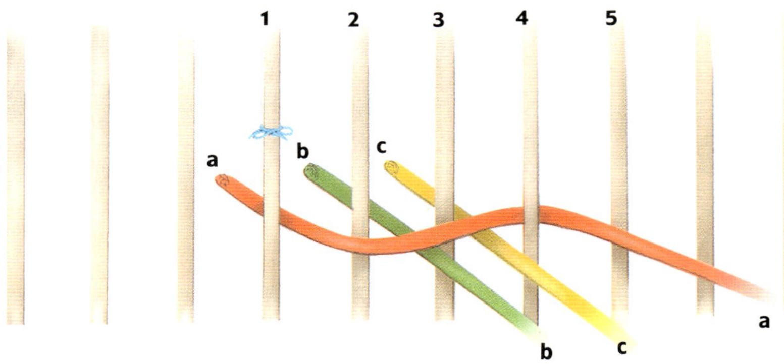

1 Lay 3 weavers (**a**, **b** and **c** in the diagram) in 3 consecutive spaces

2 Mark the spoke on the left of the left-hand weaver with a short length of string.

3 Take the left-hand weaver – **a** – in front of 2 spokes – **1** and **2** – over the top of weavers **b** and **c**, behind 1 spoke – **3** – and out to the front in the space between spokes **3** and **4**. Note that the weavers all travel in front of 2 spokes, behind 1 – **remember this rule.**

4 Then, take weaver **b**, now the left-hand weaver, in front of 2 spokes – **2** and **3** – over weavers **c** and **a**, behind 1 spoke – **4** – and out to the front between spokes **4** and **5**.

5 Take weaver **c** in front of 2 spokes – **3** and **4** – behind spoke **5** and out to the front between spokes **5** and **6**. Continue in this way, always working with the left-hand weaver.

Working a Step-up in a Three-rod Wale

When working waling weaves in round reed, it is common practice to work a "step-up" at the end of every row. This prevents the weave from spiraling.

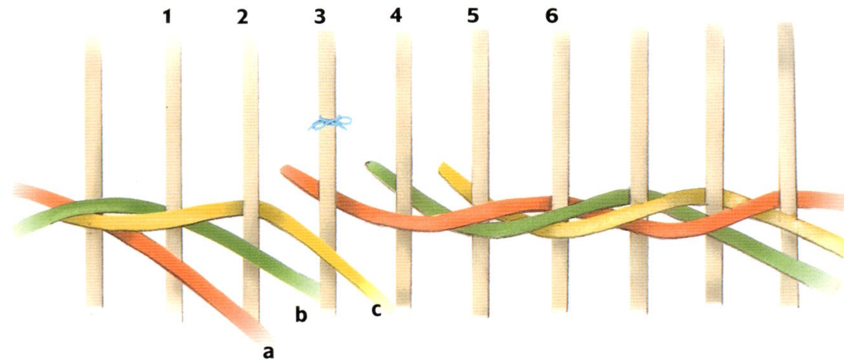

1 The diagram shows the position of the weavers just before the step-up is worked. Note that the right-hand weaver – **c** – is in the space immediately to the left of the marked spoke. For 3 strokes only, the weavers are worked in reverse order.

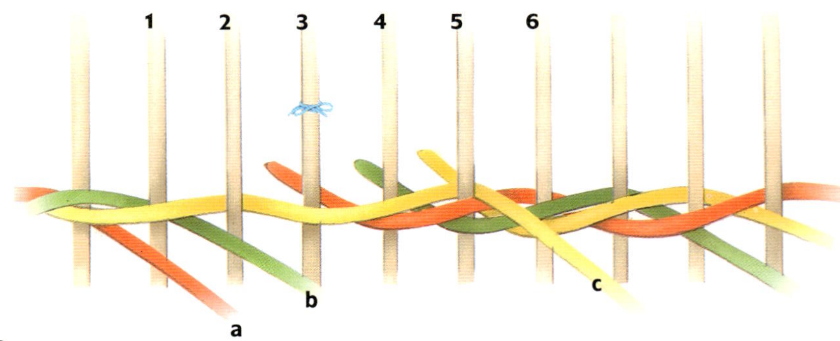

2 Take the right-hand weaver – **c** – in front of spokes **3** and **4** and behind spoke **5**.

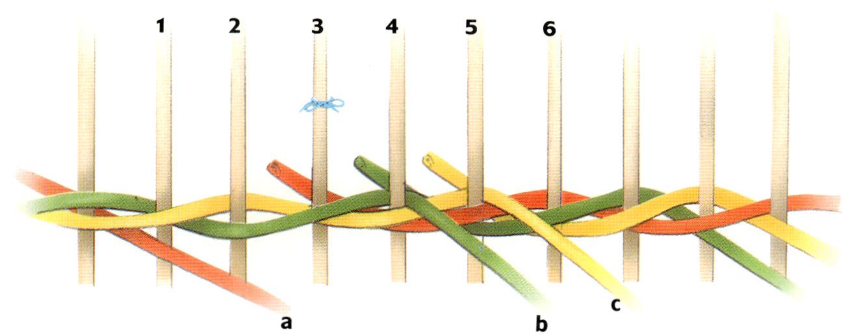

3 Take the middle weaver – **b** – in front of spokes **2** and **3** and behind spoke **4**.

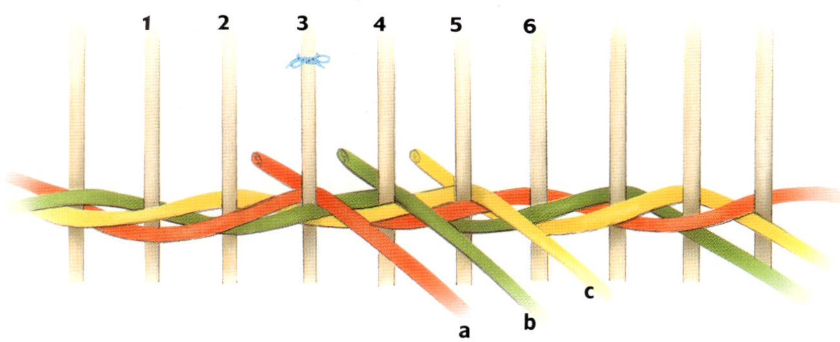

4 Take the left-hand weaver – **a** – in front of spokes **1** and **2** and behind spoke **3**. Weaver **a** now lies in the space immediately to the right of the marked spoke. The step-up is now complete. The next row of waling can now be worked as explained above, starting with the left-hand weaver – **a**.

Joining in a Three-rod Wale

1 Make sure that the weaver to be joined is the left-hand one – **A**.

2 Insert the new weaver – **a** – in the space between the old weaver – **A** – and spoke **1**, so that it lies under weavers **b** and **c**.

3 Then, continue waling as before – in front of 2 spokes and behind 1 spoke and so on. Never join at or near a step-up.

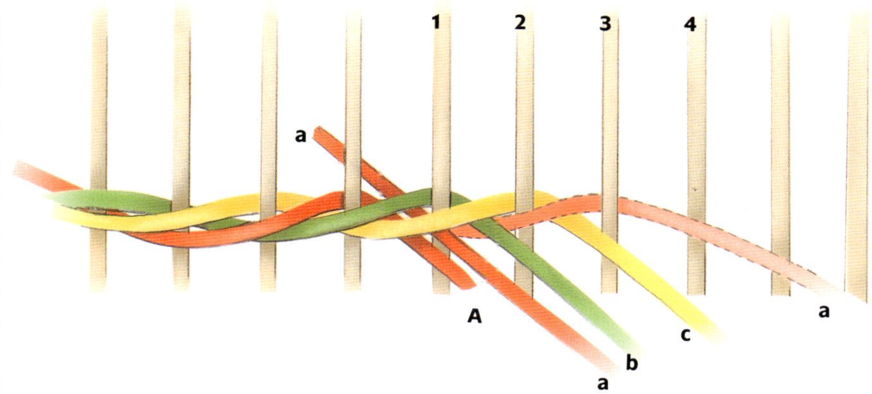

Completing a Three-rod Wale

1 Work a step-up as explained above.

2 Thread each weaver under the top 2 strands of weaving as follows:

a under **b** and **c**
b under **a** and **c**
c under **a** and **b**

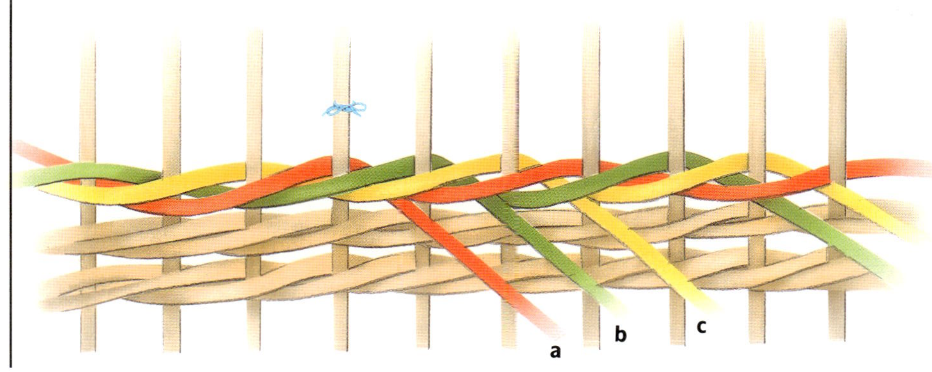

FOUR-ROD WALE

As you might expect, this weave is very similar to a three-rod wale. The difference is that the weavers travel in front of 3 spokes before going behind 1, instead of in front of 2 spokes.

Working a Step-up in a Four-rod Wale

This, too, is worked in almost the same way as for a three-rod step-up, except that there are 4 stages, with each weaver traveling in front of 3 spokes and behind 1, but in reverse order, from right to left.

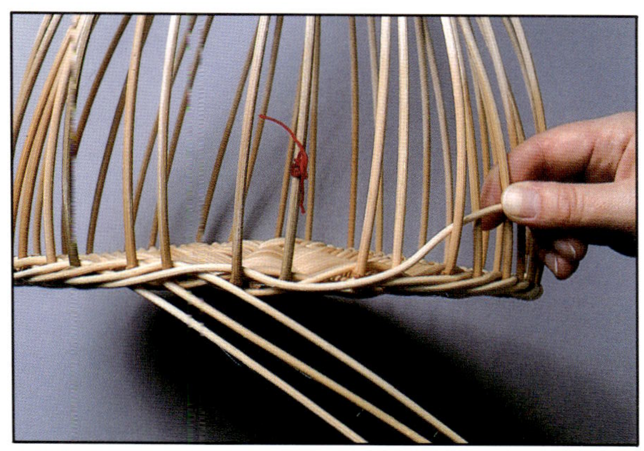

TRIMMING

Trimming ends of weavers

With the flat side of the sidecutters against the weaving, trim off the ends of the weavers left on both sides after joining (holding the cutters in this way produces a slanted cut that will lie level with the surface of the weaving). Note that it is essential that the cut end lies over a stick or spoke; otherwise, the weaving will unravel. When making a round mat, for example, do not trim the ends until the border is completed. There is a certain amount of movement during weaving, and ends that are cut too short can come undone in the process. The ends can be colored with felt-tip pens.

Trimming ends of border spokes

The ends of border spokes are trimmed in a similar way to trimming weavers. Note that the end must protrude slightly past the spoke over which it is lying so that it doesn't unravel.

STAKING UP

Done after the base of a basket has been completed, this is the process of inserting side spokes into the base.

Cut off the end of a stick close to the weaving, then insert a spoke each side of it, pushing each down into the weaving as far as it will go – use a skewer or awl to open up the channel a little if necessary. Repeat for the other sticks, but only cut off the ends of 1 or 2 sticks at a time or your weaving will unravel. Soak the staked-up base in hot water for 5 to 10 minutes. Using the round-nosed pliers, squeeze each of the spokes as close to the edges of the weaving as possible, then bend them upwards, gathering them together.

WORKING THE UPSETT

1

2

The first few rows of weaving after the staking up has been done and the spokes have been gathered up and tied together, are called the "upsett."

1 Turn the base on its side, with the bunch of spokes away from you, and insert 3 or 4 weavers – depending on whether you are going to work a three- or four-rod wale – into the channels in the weaving of the base, to the left of 3 (or 4) consecutive **spokes**. Use an awl or skewer to open up the weaving if necessary. Tie a short length of bright-colored string around the spoke immediately to the left of the left-hand weaver.

2 Keeping the base on its side, begin working a three- or four-rod wale (see above). Pull down on the weavers as you work in order to keep this first row of waling as close to the edge of the base weaving as possible. As you weave, spread out the spokes evenly around the base.

3

3 When the right-hand weaver is in the space immediately to the left of the marked spoke, work a three-rod or four-rod step-up (see above).

4 Turn the basket onto its base and put a weight inside to stop it from moving too much while you are weaving. The first few rows are critical to the final shape of the basket. If you want to achieve a cylindrical shape, make sure that you hold the spokes at 90° to the base, even out **very slightly**.

4

INSERTING BI-STAKES

Bi-stakes are generally inserted into the upsett waling on the right of a spoke. They provide added strength and rigidity. Normally, they are cut as long as the height (allowing for flow) of the sides of the basket.

CONTROLLING THE SHAPE OF A BASKET

For sides that flow gently outward, pull the spokes toward you a little as you weave, and vice versa if you want the sides to flow in. Untie the spokes only when you feel the sides are flowing in or out as you wish, but this should be done by the end of the upsett (approximately 5 rows). Bear in mind that it is you who controls the shape of the basket, by controlling the spokes with your hands and the weaving – shaping the sides needs constant control and checking! Keep the spokes straight, keep the spaces between them even, and make sure each spoke flows in or out at the same angle as the rest.

CHECKING THAT THE TOP OF A BASKET IS LEVEL

Mark a spare length of round reed at what looks like the lowest point and use it to measure the height of the basket all around. If any points are too high, gently tap them down with a skewer and retrim the bi-stakes if necessary.

VARNISHING

Varnishing a wicker basket serves two purposes: to provide a protective layer which helps to repel dirt, and to enhance and prolong the color of dyed reed. Take care not to apply the varnish too thickly – it must be carefully brushed in or it will "run" between the strands and look like glue. Always do the varnishing in a well-ventilated room. Clean brushes thoroughly with turpentine after use.

Placemat

This simple project is an excellent one when you are beginning basketry. The technique used is similar to that used for making the bases of the Cylindrical Basket and the Shopping Basket.

You will need

- ◊ The following sizes of round reed:
  No. 5 for the sticks
  No. 3½ for weaving (twining)
  No. 4 for the border spokes
- ◊ Suitable dye in 2 colors
- ◊ Mordant
- ◊ Dyeing equipment (see page 7)
- ◊ Sidecutters
- ◊ Tapemeasure
- ◊ Awl or skewer
- ◊ Large plastic bowl and warm to hot water
- ◊ Satin finish polyurethane or acrylic varnish
- ◊ Paintbrush
- ◊ Turpentine

Techniques used

- ☞ Dyeing Round Reed
- ☞ Cutting Round Reed
- ☞ Making the Slath
- ☞ Tying in the Slath
- ☞ Twining
- ☞ Adding a New Weaver
- ☞ Completing Twining
- ☞ Trimming
- ☞ Varnishing

See pages 6 to 13

1

1 *Dye* most of the No. 3½ round reed in 2 colors. *Cut* 8 sticks, each 10¼ inches long, from the No. 5 reed. Soak the sticks in the water for 5 to 10 minutes to soften them.

2

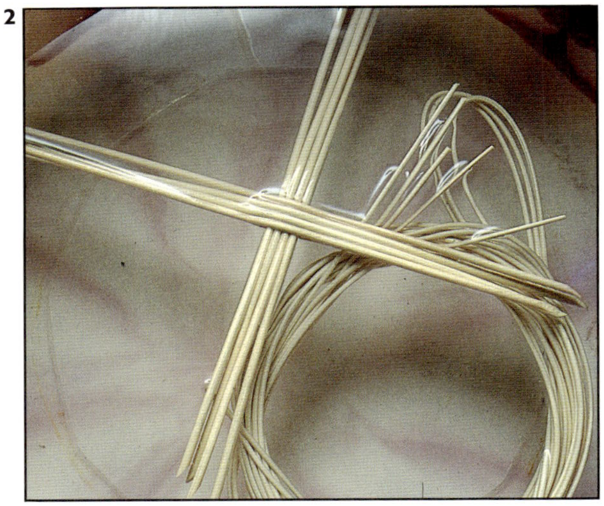

2 *Make a slath*, 4 through 4, with the sticks. Soak the slath and the No. 3½ cane in the water for 5 to 10 minutes to soften them.

3

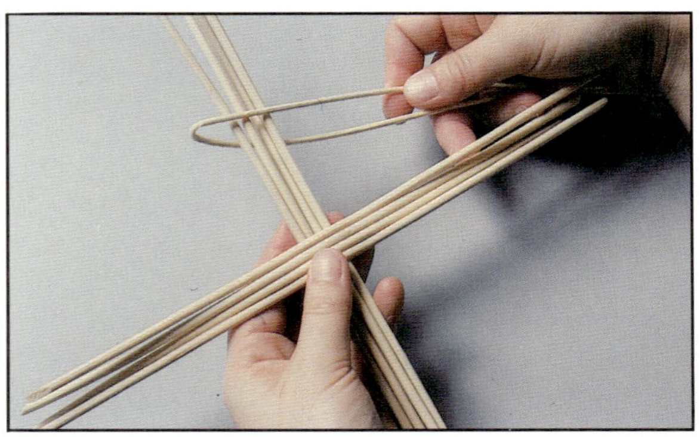

3 Take a length of undyed No. 3½ round reed. *Tie in the slath* with 3 rows of *twining*. Open out the sticks into pairs and work 2 rows, then open out the sticks into singles and work 2 rows.

4

4 You will now have worked 7 rows of twining. Your sticks should be evenly spaced. Change from natural to colored weavers by *adding* 2 lengths of dyed No. 3½ reed.

5

5 Continue twining, keeping the sticks evenly spaced. Remember, too, that the mat will need to lie flat on a table, so keep checking that the sticks remain level.

6
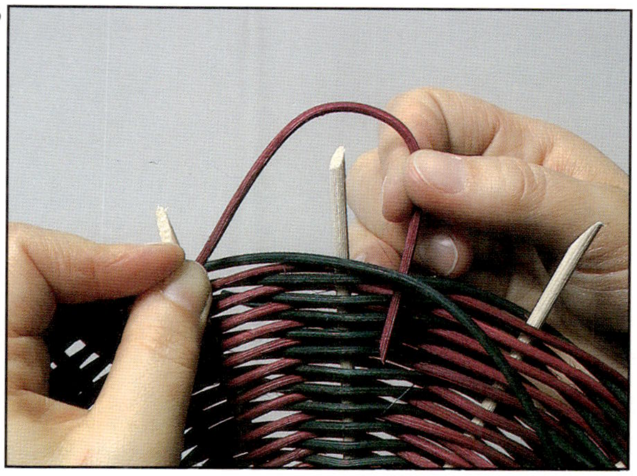

6 Dampen the mat from time to time. Continue twining for 15 rows, then *complete the twining*.

7
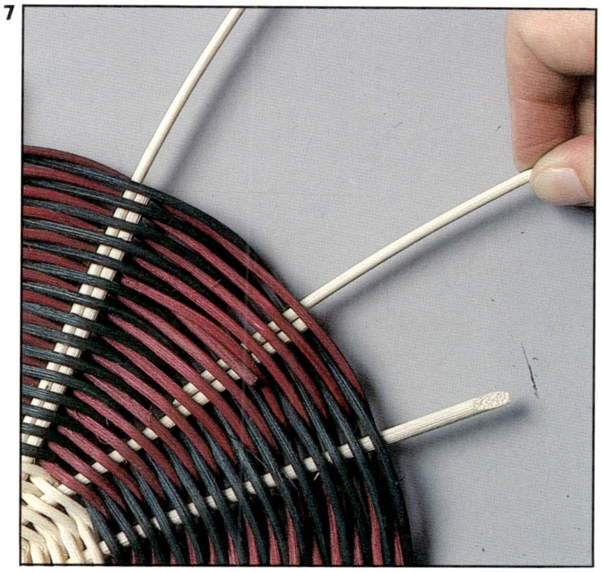

7 Cut 16 border spokes from the No. 4 reed, each 13½ inches long. With the right side of the mat facing, cut off the end of a stick close to the weaving – the side facing you as you work – then insert a border spoke to the left-hand side of the stick, pushing it down into the weaving to where the dyed weaving begins. If necessary, use the awl to open up the weaving a little to make inserting the spoke easier. Insert the remaining border spokes in the same way, but cut off only 1 or 2 sticks at a time, or your weaving will unravel.

8

8 Soak the border spokes. With the right side facing, work the first stage of the border. Carefully bend a spoke down to the right and weave it in front of the next spoke, behind the next, and back to the front.

9

9 Continue this process with each border spoke. The last few border spokes need to be threaded through the spokes already worked. Be careful to maintain the same sequence by looking closely at the pattern created by the border so far.

10
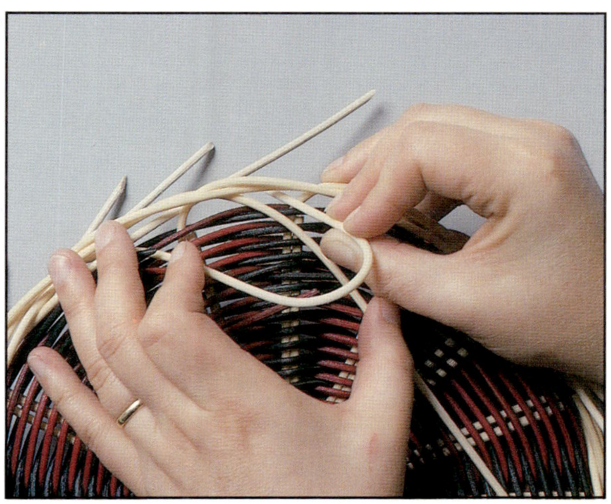

10 To complete the border, work the end of each spoke in front of the spoke to the right of it (imagine the spoke is still standing upright) and over the end of the spoke sticking out on the right. Thread it through to the back, just to the left of the second spoke along to the right, between the last row of the colored weaving and the border. The end will now lie behind this second spoke to the right. Repeat with every spoke, maintaining the pattern when working the last 2 spokes.

11 *Trim* the ends of the weavers left on both sides of the mat after joining. With the wrong side of the mat facing, trim the ends of the border stakes in a similar way. Finally, give the mat a coat of *varnish*.

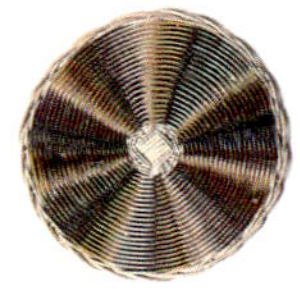

Tablemat

This is a slightly larger and thicker mat than the Placemat in the previous project and introduces a new weave. You can use this mat as a placemat or to protect the table under hot dishes. The main weave – a three-rod wale – produces a striking, radiating pattern when worked in three colors over a number of spokes divisible by 3 – essential to achieve this pattern.

What you need

◊ The following sizes of round reed:

No. 5½ for the sticks
No. 3½ for weaving (twining and waling)
No. 5 for the border spokes

◊ Suitable dye in 2 colors
◊ Mordant
◊ Dyeing equipment (see page 7)
◊ Sidecutters
◊ Tapemeasure
◊ Awl or skewer
◊ Large plastic bowl with warm to hot water
◊ Satin finish polyurethane or acrylic varnish
◊ Paintbrush
◊ Turpentine

Techniques used

☞ Dyeing Round Reed
☞ Cutting Round Reed
☞ Making the Slath
☞ Tying in the Slath
☞ Twining
☞ Adding a New Weaver
☞ Three-rod Wale
☞ Working a Step-up in a Three-rod Wale
☞ Joining in a Three-rod Wale
☞ Completing a Three-rod Wale
☞ Trimming
☞ Varnishing
See pages 6 to 13

1

1 *Dye* just under ⅓ of the No. 3½ round reed in one of the colors and the same amount in the other color. *Cut* 10 sticks, each 14¼ inches long, from the No. 5½ reed and soak them. Pierce 5 of them through the center.

2

2 *Make a slath*, threading 5 sticks through 5 sticks. Soak the slath and the undyed No. 3½ reed for 5 to 10 minutes to soften them. *Tie in the slath* with 2 rows of *twining*, using a length of undyed No. 3½ round reed.

3

3 On the third row, open out the sticks to give 3 groups of sticks each opened out as follows: a pair on the left, a single in the middle, and a pair on the right.

4

4 *Complete the twining* at the end of the next row – 4 rows in total.

5

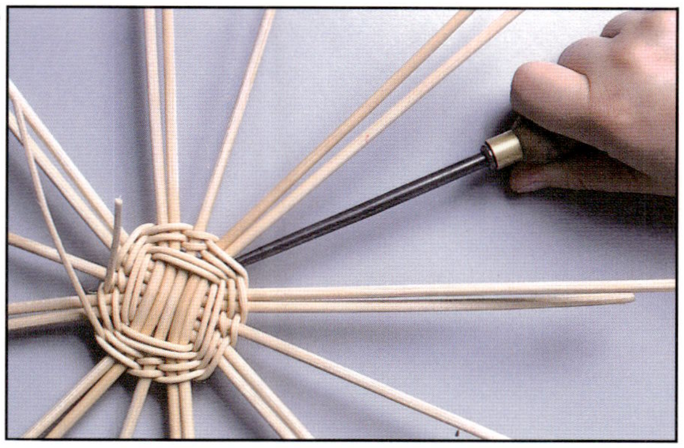

5 On the right-hand side of a pair of sticks, insert the awl to open up a channel in the weaving.

6

6 Cut an extra stick, 6 inches long, from the No. 5½ round reed and insert it into the channel you have made, pushing it down as far as it will go. This gives a total of 21 sticks – a number divisible by 3, which is necessary in order for the 3-color pattern to work. Soak some undyed and dyed No. 3½ reed.

7

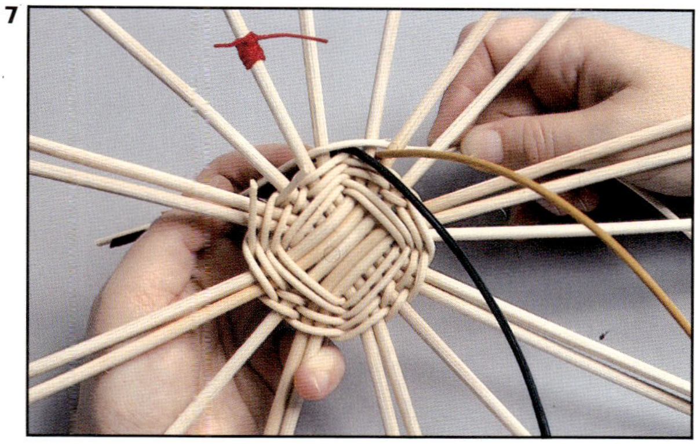

7 Spread out the sticks into singles. Lay 3 No. 3½ weavers – 1 natural and 1 of each dyed color in 3 consecutive spaces. Tie a marker onto the spoke on the left of the left-hand weaver. Don't begin waling near the extra stick inserted in step 6.

8

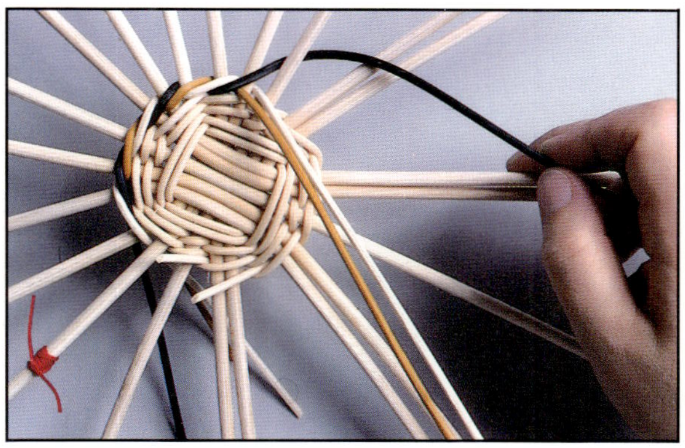

8 Begin a *three-rod wale*. At the same time as you weave, open out the sticks into singles.

9

9 When working a wale in round reed, it is usual to work a *step-up* at the end of every row so that each row is completed, preventing the weave from spiraling. Now work a step-up.

10

10 Begin the second row as before, starting with the left-hand weaver. Continue, working a step-up at the end of each row. When you need to, *add new weavers*, but **don't** join at or near a step-up. Work 20 rows of three-rod waling altogether. Work a step-up at the end of the last row, then *complete the three-rod wale*.

11

11 Cut 21 border spokes from No. 5 round reed, each 13½ inches long. With the wrong side of the mat facing, use the sidecutters to cut off the end of a stick close to the weaving. Insert a border spoke into the channel in the weaving on the right of the stick (use the awl to open it a little if necessary), pushing the spoke down to where the 3-rod wale started. Insert the remaining border spokes in the same way, but only cut off 1 or 2 sticks at a time, or your weaving will unravel.

12

12 Soak the border spokes. With the right side facing, work the first stage of the border. Carefully bend a spoke down to the right and weave it in front of the next spoke, behind the next, and back to the front.

13

13 Continue this process with each border spoke. The last few border spokes need to be threaded through the stakes already worked. Be careful to maintain the same sequence by looking closely at the pattern created by the border so far.

14

14 To complete the border, work the end of each spoke in front of the spoke on the right of it (imagine the spoke is still standing upright) and over the end of the spoke sticking out to the right. Thread it through to the back, just to the left of the second stake along to the right, between the last row of the colored weaving and the border. The end will now lie behind this second spoke on the right. Repeat with every spoke, maintaining the pattern when working the last 2 stakes.

15

15 *Trim* the ends of the weavers left on both sides of the mat after joining.

16

16 *Trim the ends* of the border spokes in a similar way. Take care not to cut the ends too short or the weaving will unravel. Finally, *varnish* the mat to protect it.

Cylindrical Basket

A versatile basket that could be equally useful as a container for a potted plant or for waste paper. While introducing new skills, this project builds on those learned in the previous two projects and combines all the techniques learned so far. If you like, you can easily plot alternative colored patterns on graph paper.

You will need

- ◊ The following sizes of round reed:

No. 5½ for the sticks
No. 3½ for weaving (twining and waling)
No. 4 for the spokes and bi-stakes

- ◊ Suitable dye in 4 colors: dark brown, dusty pink, dark yellow, and orange
- ◊ Mordant
- ◊ Dyeing equipment (see page 7)
- ◊ Sidecutters
- ◊ Tapemeasure
- ◊ Awl or skewer
- ◊ Round-nosed pliers
- ◊ String
- ◊ Weight
- ◊ Large plastic bowl and warm to hot water
- ◊ Satin finish polyurethane or acrylic varnish
- ◊ Paintbrush
- ◊ Turpentine
- ◊ Graph paper and colored pencils

Techniques used

- ☞ Dyeing Round Reed
- ☞ Cutting Round Reed
- ☞ Making the Slath
- ☞ Tying in the Slath
- ☞ Twining
- ☞ Adding a New Weaver
- ☞ Completing the Twining
- ☞ Three-rod waling
- ☞ Working a Step-up in a Three-rod Wale
- ☞ Joining in a Three-rod Wale
- ☞ Staking up
- ☞ Working the Upsett
- ☞ Completing Waling
- ☞ Trimming
- ☞ Checking that the Top of a Basket is Level
- ☞ Varnishing

See pages 6 to 13

WEAVE PATTERN CHART

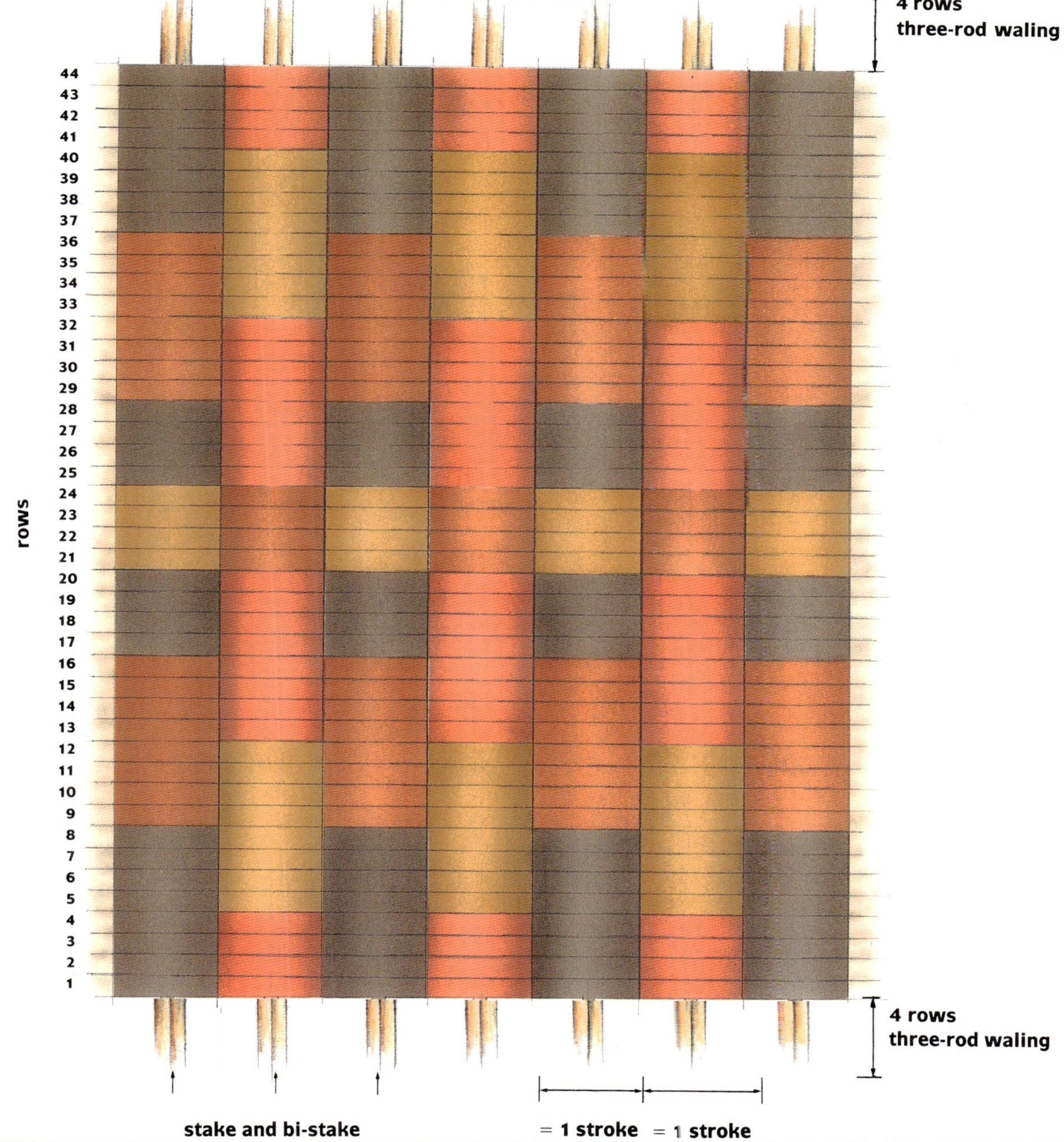

1

2

3

1 *Dye* most of the No. 3½ round reed in the 4 colors. *Cut* 8 sticks, each 12½ inches long, from the No. 5½ reed. Soak the sticks in the water for 5 to 10 minutes to soften them. *Make a 4-through-4 slath* with the sticks. Soak the slath and some undyed No. 3½ reed in the water. Take a length of No. 3½ reed and *tie in the slath* with 2 rows of *twining*. On the 3rd row, open out the sticks to pairs.

2 Work 2 rows with the sticks in pairs, then open out the sticks to singles and continue pairing until the diameter is about 9 inches. At the same time, while weaving, gently push the sticks away from you to create a **very slightly** domed shape – like a shallow saucer. *Complete the twining.*

3 Cut 32 stakes, each 24½ inches long, from the No. 4 round reed. *Stake up* the base by inserting a spoke on each side of each base stick, pushing each one down as far as it will go, using the awl, if necessary, to open a channel in the weaving. Then soak the staked-up base and some undyed No. 5 cane in water for 5–10 minutes.

4

5

6

4 Using the round-nosed pliers, squeeze each of the spokes as close to the edge of the base weaving as possible, then carefully bend them up, gathering them together in your hand as you go.

5 Cut a length of string and tie up the spokes in a bunch about 12 inches above the base, keeping the bunch located centrally over the base. *Start the upsett*, with 3 soaked undyed No. 3½ cane weavers. After the first row, turn the basket onto its base and put the weight on it, to anchor it down. Work a total of 5 rows of *three-rod waling* for the *upsett*, then *complete the waling* and untie the stakes.

6 Cut 32 bi-stakes, each 11½ inches long, from the No. 4 cane. *Insert a bi-stake* into the waling on the right-hand side of every spoke.

7

7 Now begin weaving the sides. Lay 1 dark brown No. 3½ round reed weaver in 1 space and 1 dusty pink No. 3½ weaver in the next space and twine for 4 rows.

8 At the end of the 4th row *join in* a dark yellow No. 3½ weaver in place of the dusty pink one and continue twining for 4 more rows.

8

9

9 Join in an orange No. 3½ round reed weaver in place of the brown one and continue weaving in the same way, changing the colors of the weavers as indicated on the chart, until you have worked 44 rows of twining altogether. As you weave, *trim* the ends of the weavers on the inside of the basket as you go, but leave the ends on the outside as they are. Also, constantly *check the shape of the basket*. If it is beginning to flow inward or outward, it is worth undoing a few rows of weaving at this stage, to correct the shape, rather than being dissatisfied with the end result.

10

10 Lay 3 undyed No. 3½ round reed weavers in 3 consecutive spaces and mark the step-up by tying a short length of string to the spoke immediately on the left of the left-hand weaver. Begin a three-rod wale.

11

11 Remembering to work a *step-up* at the end of each row, work 4 rows.

12

12 *Complete the waling*. Remove the marker.

13

13 With the flat side of the sidecutters pressing down slightly on the weaving, cut off the remaining ends of the bi-stakes. *Check that the top of the basket is level* – trimming bi-stakes, if necessary. Soak the spokes well in the water.

14

14 Next, work the first stage of the border. Bring each upright spoke down to the right and weave it in front of 2 upright spokes and behind 1 upright spoke. Leave the spoke on the inside of the basket. Take the next spoke to the right and weave it in front of 2 spokes and behind 1 and so on until you get to the last 2 spokes.

15 To work the last 2 upright spokes, first bring the left-hand spoke down to the right in front of the 1 remaining upright spoke and in front of and under the spoke on the right, to lie behind the second spoke that was brought down. Finally bring the last upright spoke down in front of and under the 2 spokes on its right to lie behind the third spoke that was brought down. All ends should now be on the inside of the basket.

15

16

16 To work the second stage of the border, bring each spoke back to the outside by bringing each spoke end over the 2 spoke ends on its right, and then to the outside by threading it between the side weaving and the border.

17

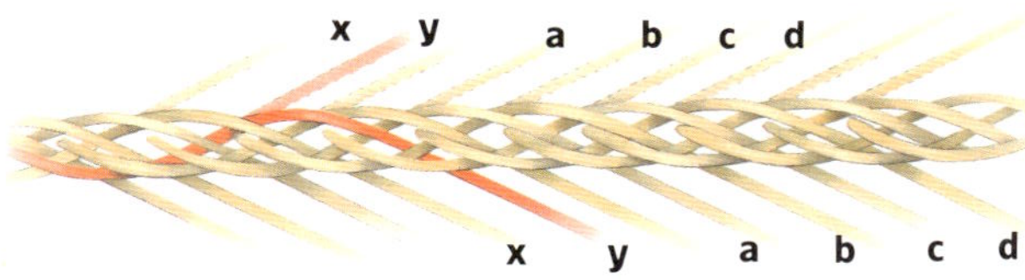

17 When only 2 spokes **x** and **y** remain on the inside, take the lefthand spoke, **x**, and work it behind two spokes (**b** and **c** – imagine them still upright), over the last spoke remaining on the inside – **y**, and then to the outside between the side weaving and the border. Finally, take the last spoke **y** behind two spokes (**c** and **d** – imagine them upright), over **a** and **b** (imagine them still on the inside) and thread **y** to the outside between the border (i.e. under **c** and **d** and the side weaving).

18

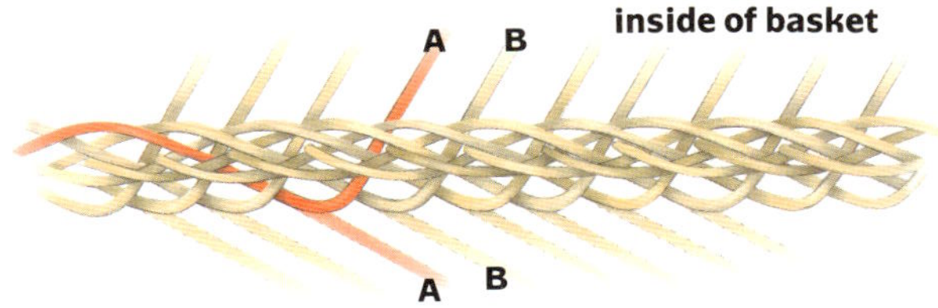

18 To work the final stage of the border, take each spoke to the inside of the basket again by taking each one in front of the 2 spokes immediately to the right of it (imagine the spokes standing upright), over the spoke sticking out immediately to its right, then through to the back between the weaving and the border to lie behind the third spoke along on the right.

19

19 When you are certain that the border is correct, trim the ends of the border spokes. It is better to trim these ends so that they are a fraction too long rather than cut them too short. Trim the ends of the weavers on the outside of the basket. *Varnish* the basket inside and out.

Shopping Basket

It would be a shame to carry only potatoes in this wonderfully colorful basket – a few red peppers, a yellow melon, green apples, and some eggplants would be much more in keeping with its cheerful colors.

You will need

- ◊ The following sizes of round reed:
  No. 5½ for the sticks
  No. 5 for the spokes and bi-stakes
  No. 4 for the four-rod waling
  No. 3½ for the three-rod waling and twining
  Handle reed for the border core, handle liners, and handle
- ◊ Suitable dye in 4 colors: green, turquoise, red, and yellow
- ◊ Mordant
- ◊ Dyeing equipment (see page 7)
- ◊ Sidecutters
- ◊ Tapemeasure
- ◊ Awl or skewer
- ◊ String
- ◊ Weight
- ◊ Round-nosed pliers
- ◊ Craft knife
- ◊ Large plastic bowl and warm to hot water
- ◊ Satin finish polyurethane or acrylic varnish
- ◊ Paintbrush
- ◊ Turpentine
- ◊ Graph paper and colored pencils

Techniques used

- ☞ Dyeing Round Reed
- ☞ Cutting Round Reed
- ☞ Making the Slath
- ☞ Tying in the Slath
- ☞ Twining
- ☞ Joining in a New Weaver in pairing
- ☞ Four-rod Wale
- ☞ Working a Step-up in a Four-rod Wale
- ☞ Three-rod Wale
- ☞ Working a Step-up in a Three-rod Wale
- ☞ Completing a Three-rod and Four-rod Wale
- ☞ Checking That the Top of a Basket is Level
- ☞ Trimming
- ☞ Varnishing

See pages 6 to 13

1
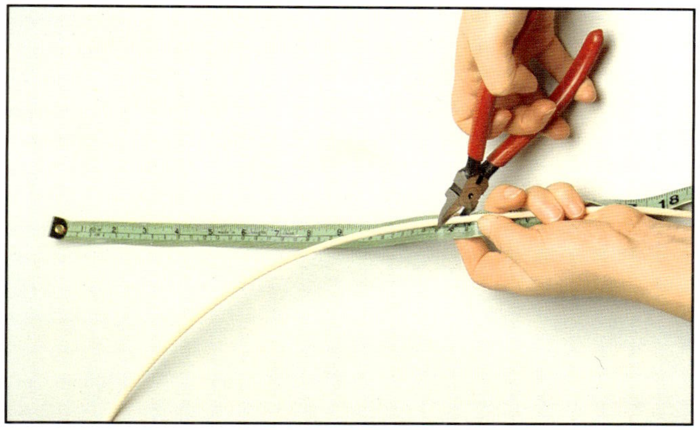

1 *Dye* most of the No. 3½ round reed in the 4 colors. *Cut* 9 sticks 12½ inches long, from the No. 5½ reed. Soak the sticks in the water for 5 to 10 minutes to soften them.

2

2 *Make a five through four slath* with the sticks, threading 5 sticks through 4. Soak the slath and the undyed No. 3½ round reed in the water for 5 to 10 minutes to soften them.

3
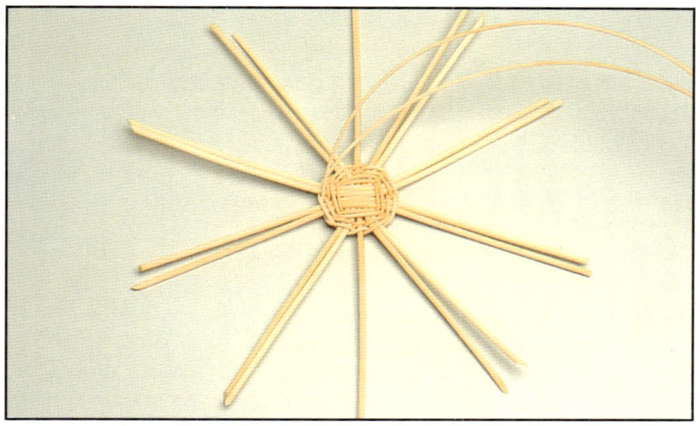

3 Take a length of No. 3½ round reed and *tie in the slath* with 2 rows of *twining*. On the third row, begin opening out the sticks as follows: the groups of 4 into pairs and the groups of 5 into a pair, a single and a pair. N.B. Keep the central, single, sticks in the groups of 5 straight.

4
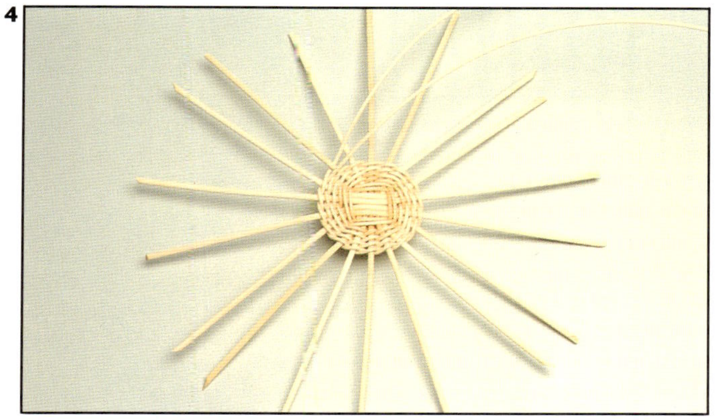

4 On the 5th row, open out the sticks to singles. Make sure that you keep the 2 singles of step 2 straight. This is important; later, they act as guides for the positioning of the handle. Continue twining until the diameter is about 8¾ inches. As you work, gently push the sticks away from you to create a **very slightly** domed shape, like a shallow saucer. *Complete the twining.* The base will be slightly oval in shape due to the number of sticks used in the slath. Cut 36 stakes 23½ inches long, from No. 5 round reed.

5

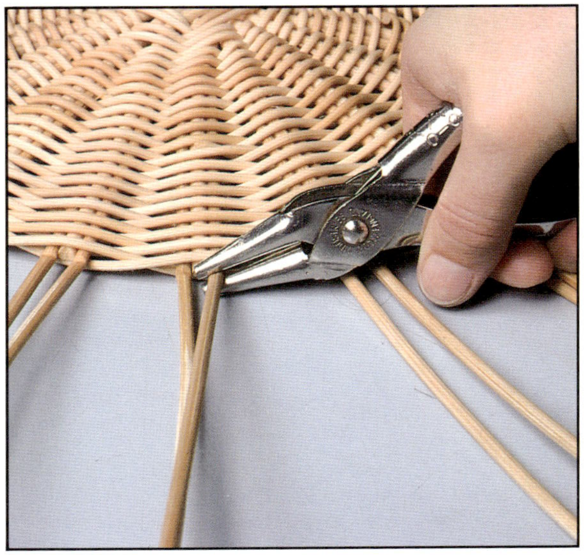

5 *Stake up the base* by inserting a spoke on each side of each base stick, pushing each one down as far as it will go, using the awl if necessary, to open up the space in the weaving. Soak the staked-up base in hot water for 5 to 10 minutes. Using the round-nosed pliers, squeeze each of the spokes as close to the edge of the weaving as possible, then carefully bend them up, gathering them together in your hand as you squeeze each spoke.

6

6 Cut a length of string and tie up the spokes in a bunch about 12 inches above the base. Insert 4 soaked, undyed No. 4 weavers into the base, weaving to the left of 4 consecutive spokes. Remember to mark the spoke on the left of the left-hand weaver. Begin *working the upsett* using a *four-rod wale*. Work a *four-rod step-up* at the end of each row.

7

7 After the first row, turn the basket onto its base, put a weight on its base, and pull the spokes toward you as you weave so that the sides of the basket begin to flow gently outward. At the end of the third row, untie the spokes – they should now be leaning out at the angle you want the sides of the finished basket to be. *Complete the four-rod wale* at the end of the fifth row.

8

8 Cut 36 bi-stakes 8¾ inches long, from No. 5 round reed. Insert 1 to the right of each spoke.

9

9 Lay in 3 soaked No. 3½ weavers in green, blue, and red, in 3 consecutive spaces, but not directly above where the four-rod wale ended.

Begin working a *three-rod wale*, marking the spoke on the left of the left-hand weaver to mark the step-up.

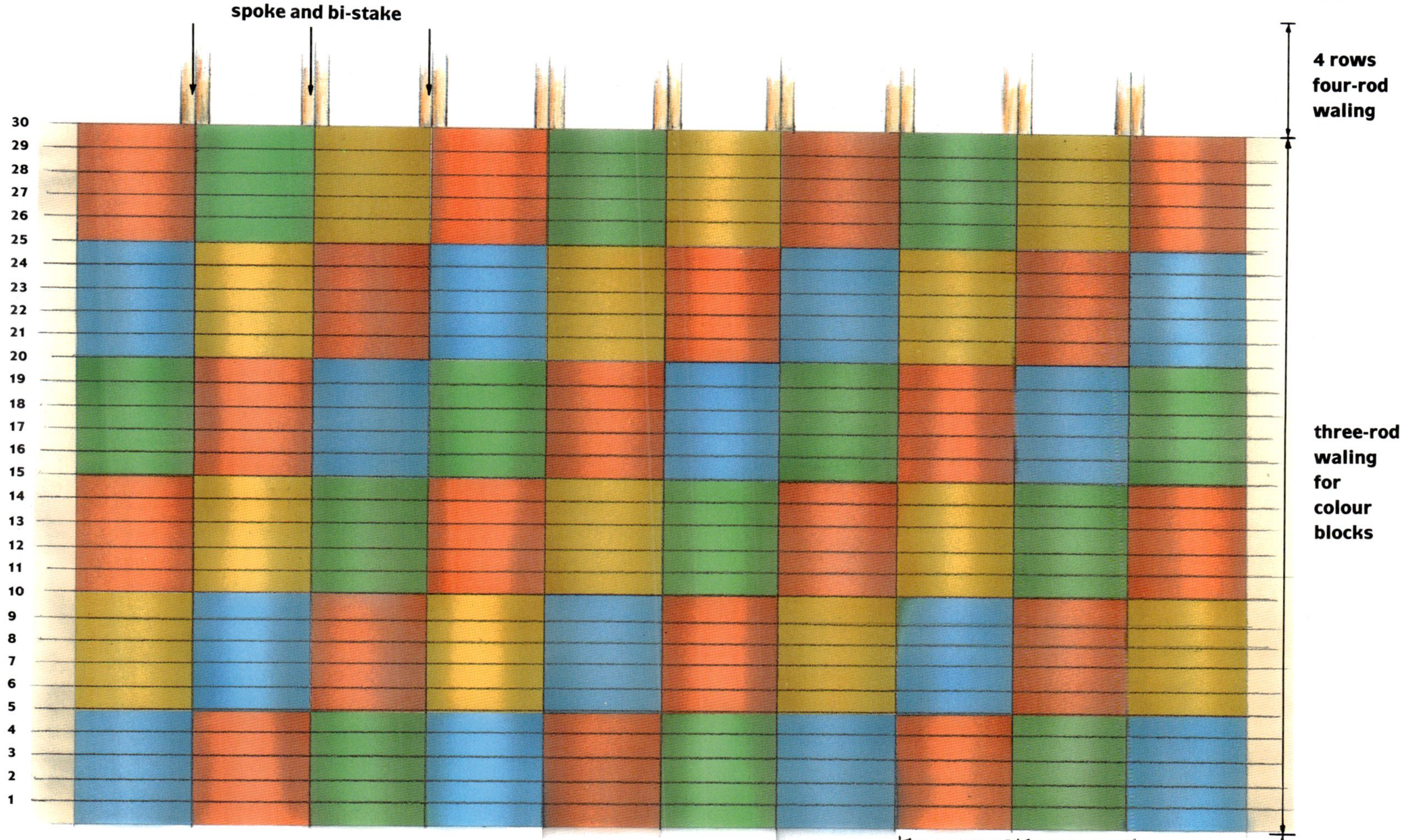

WEAVE PATTERN CHART

10 Work 5 rows, with a *step-up* at the end of each row. *Complete the waling.* Starting in a different place, lay in 3 new No. 3½ weavers in consecutive spaces as follows: red where the green was, blue where the red was, yellow where the blue was. Mark where the new step-up will occur and remember to work one at the end of every row. At the end of the next 5 rows, complete this block of waling as before. Start the third block of waling in another place – remember to mark the step-up – and refer to the pattern chart to see which color weaver goes where.

10

11

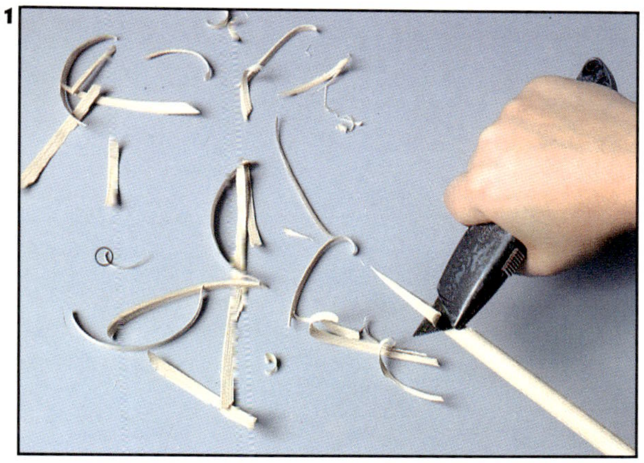

11 When the third block of waling has been worked, make and insert the handle liners (the markers) by cutting 2 lengths of handle reed, each about 12 inches long, and use the craft knife to cut one end of each length to a two-sided point about 2–2½ inches long.

12 Look at the base of the basket and note where the oval is narrower across the middle. See where the central stick of the group of 5 sticks passed through the 4 in the slath and follow it out across the base of the basket (see the photo detail). Each end of this stick will carry 2 spokes. Push the handle liner down into the channel to one side of one of these spokes – the most central one – as far as it will go, to the bottom if possible. Find the corresponding spokes on the opposite side and insert the second handle liner. Check the positioning of the handle liners from above.

12

13 To emphasize the oval shape of the basket, thread a long piece of strong string through the weaving from one side to the other, around the outside, back through and out the other side, and tie the ends together tightly. The handle liners need to be opposite each other across the narrowest part of the oval as shown in the diagram. Check that the oval the string creates is the shape you desire – but not too extreme – adjusting the string now if necessary.

13

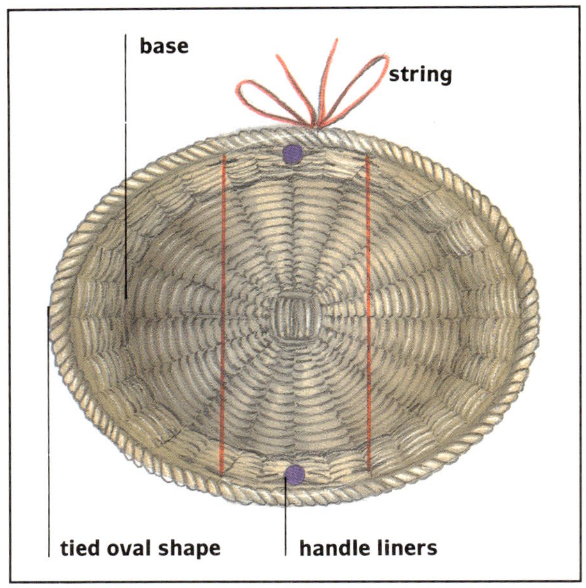

14 Continue working the blocks of three-rod wale as before, treating the handle liner and spoke it is next to as one, referring to the chart. Remember to *control the shape of the basket* all the time and to begin each block of color pattern in a different place and to mark and *work the step-up*. After the sixth and last color block, complete the three-rod waling. Lay in 4 soaked, undyed No. 4 weavers into 4 consecutive spaces.

15 Work 4 rows of four-rod waling, working a four-rod step-up at the end of each row. Complete the four-rod waling.

14

15

16

16 *Trim* the bi-stakes (take care not to cut the spokes) and *check that the top of the basket is level* – re-trimming bi-stakes if necessary. Soak the spokes well. Then, with the round-nosed pliers resting lightly on the side weaving, pinch each spoke.

17

17 Cut a length of handle reed about 8 inches longer than the circumference of the top rim of the basket. This is to be the border core. Using the craft knife, shave one side of one end of the border core for about 3½ inches. Hold the border core outside the top edge of the basket in front of a handle liner, and with the shaved end facing you. The rest of the border core should be lying on the right. Tie it to the handle liner with a piece of string.

18

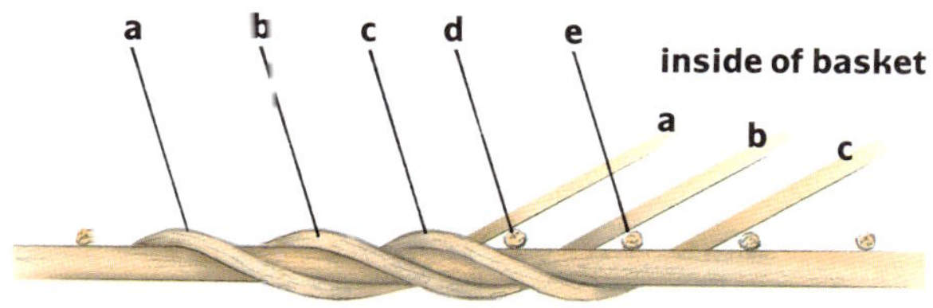

18 Next, work the first stage of the border. Spoke **a** is brought down to the right, in front of spokes **b** and **c**, over the core, then threaded under the core to lie behind spoke **d**. Spoke **b** is then brought down to the right, in front of **c** and **d**, over the core. It is then threaded under the core to lie behind spoke **e**, and so on, until all the spokes are on the inside of the basket.

19

19 When you have gone almost all the way around, trim and shave the other end of the border core on the inside, to match the other end as closely as possible so that the 2 ends lie together as one. Remove the string and re-tie, holding both ends together and to the handle liner, and complete stage one of the border, working over the joined border cane to secure it. Take care to maintain the pattern sequence.

20

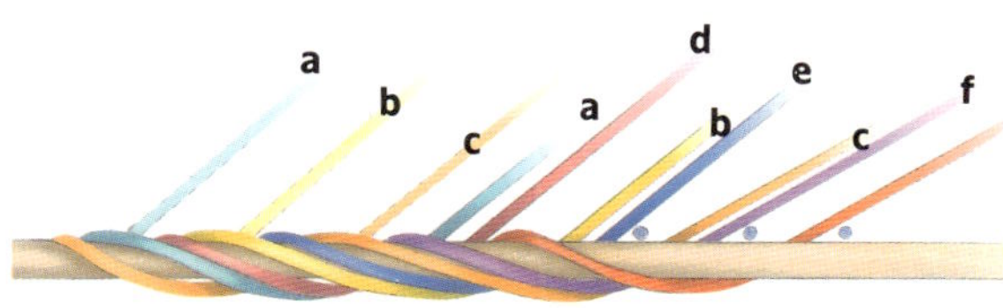

20 The second stage of the border is worked by bringing each spoke back up and over the core again, each spoke following the path of the spoke to its right. Take **a** and bring it back over the core again following, on the left-hand side, the path of **d**. Then thread it back to the inside again between the side weaving and the border. **a** will now be lying to the left of **d**, forming a pair. Repeat with **b** and then **c**, so that they form pairs with **e** and **f** respectively. Continue this process until all the strands are back to being singles, coming out of consecutive spaces all around the basket.

21

inside of basket

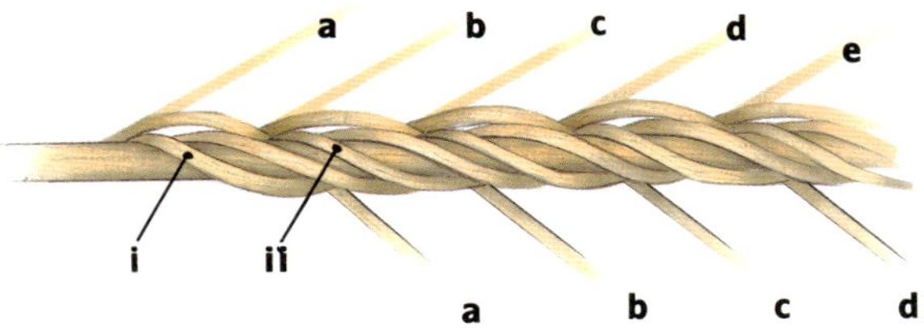

21 Finally, take all the ends to the outside by taking each strand to the right, behind a spoke (imagine it upright), over the end immediately to its right, and thread it to the outside between the side weaving and the border, just before the next spoke along, which it will rest against. So take **a** behind **i**, over **b**, under the border to the outside just before **ii**. Take all the ends to the outside in the same way.

22

22 Check that the pattern sequence created by the border is correct and the tension is even, then trim the ends of the border spokes and weavers. Leave the basket to dry.

23 Cut a length of handle reed about 35–37 inches long to make the handle "bow." Using the craft knife, shave one end to a two-sided point 2–2½ inches long. Briefly soak the handle bow to prevent it from becoming brittle. Remove 1 handle liner and push the pointed end of the handle bow into the same channel in the weaving **with the cut side in**. Carefully bend the handle bow over the top of the basket and measure how long it needs to be. Allow for it to curve – about 5½–6 inches above the border at its maximum height – and

23

to go right down into the weaving on the other side. Cut it to the right length and shave the end to a point as for the other end. Remove the other handle liner and push the end of the handle bow firmly down into the channel in the weaving. Adjust the shape of the handle until you have a good, even curve.

24

24 The handle is now pegged to secure it. Cut 2 short lengths of No. 5 round reed. Push the awl right through the handle between the second and third rows of the four-rod wale.

25

25 Quickly insert 1 of the pieces of No. 5 round reed into the hole and, keeping in mind the purpose of the peg, trim off the ends by laying the flat side of the sidecutters against the weaving when cutting. Repeat this on the other side.

26

26 To cover the handle bow, take 4 or 5 strands of the dyed No. 3½ round reed, 5 times the length of the handle, and thread them through the weaving on the left of the handle between the three- and four-rod waling. Pull the ends through to the inside until you have 1½ times the length of the handle. Take the ends on the outside of the basket diagonally up across the handle and, wrap them around the handle 3 or 4 times, leaving equal-sized gaps between the "bands" of colored reed.

27

28

29

27 When you reach the other side, take the strands diagonally down across the handle and thread the ends through to the inside between the three- and four-rod waling as before. Both ends of the handle should look the same, with the diagonal band of round reed going from top right to bottom left. Then bring the ends of the reed on the inside up and to the front, keeping to the left of the handle bow. Wind them back over the handle, laying the new band of round reed in the gap above the first. When you reach the other side, leave the strands on the inside. Repeat this procedure using the long strands of reed remaining on the inside of the opposite side.

28 After wrapping the handle, if there are still some small gaps – "grins" – take another strand of dyed No. 3½ reed and wind it along the path where the grins are. The ends of this strand of reed lie with both groups of ends left on the inside from the previous stages. There may still be some very small grins on top of the handle, but it is best to leave these as the curve on the top of the handle bow is longer than that underneath.

29 To bind each end of the handle, insert a length of No 3½ reed down to the right side of the handle bow. Bring it to the outside and wrap it clockwise around the handle 5 or 6 times, as tightly as possible. Thread the end back down through the binding, following the same diagonal as the reed wound around the handle and using an awl if necessary to create enough room to do this. Then pull the end down to tighten the binding, leaving it on the back of the handle. Repeat this on the opposite side of the basket.

30 Using the sidecutters, carefully trim the ends of the cane used to wrap and bind the handle so that they lie against the inside of the border and top rows of waling. *Varnish* the basket inside and out.

CHAPTER 2

USING CARDBOARD

INTRODUCTION

Some of the best cardboard boxes to use are those that have been used to deliver cereal to shops and supermarkets. Potato chip boxes can also be used, but they are often made from low-quality cardboard that tends to tear easily, and some have a perforated shape in one side to be pressed out so stores can display them for customers to serve themselves – which means that you will need more boxes. Large boxes that have been used for, say, packing a shower unit or radiator are ideal.

If you ask at a neighborhood store, more often than not they will keep a few suitable boxes aside for you to collect. Otherwise, some supermarkets have them near the checkouts for customers to use. Early morning is a good time to go as there is usually a better selection then. The two most important qualities to look for when selecting boxes are:

size the circumference must be sufficient to produce strips of the length required. The number of boxes you will need to collect to give the right number of strips will depend on the height of the boxes.

type of cardboard the cardboard must be corrugated, but with only a single layer of corrugations as those with a double layer are too stiff to weave with. If possible, especially for your first few baskets, choose boxes of a similar type in terms of thickness and malleability (as a rough guide, the cardboard should be no thicker than 1/8 inch). Ideally, boxes should be identical.

Once you have collected your boxes, open them up along the seam, which will be in one corner. Flatten each box and cut off the top and bottom flaps, leaving a large rectangle of cardboard.

Next, paint one (or both) sides of the cardboard. Large, bold, colorful, random designs often work well. Bear in mind that the sheets will be cut up and woven, mixing up all the elements of your original pattern in a completely random and unexpected way. As for the colors you choose, be inspired, for example, by the home for your basket.

THE TECHNIQUES YOU NEED TO KNOW

The projects that follow have a number of techniques in common, and they are explained below. The techniques used in any one project are listed beneath the materials, and references to them in the step-by-step instructions are printed in *italics*. Until you are familiar with the techniques, it is best to read the relevant sections below before starting a project, in order to produce the best results. There are valuable tips and clear explanations that, to avoid repetition, are not described in such detail in the projects.

Preparing Cardboard Strips for Weaving

There are several important points to remember before you cut the prepared cardboard into strips:

◊ it is essential to cut *across* the corrugations as, otherwise, the strips will be virtually impossible to fold or bend
◊ measure and draw your strips very carefully to make them easier to work with and to produce a regular-shaped basket.

1 Using a ruler and a long straightedge, mark and rule the lines for the strips on the cardboard. Cut carefully along the lines with a pair of strong, sharp scissors, keeping the edges of the strips as straight as possible.

2 If there are any weak points in your strips, such as split corner creases, neatly "bandage" them using good-quality clear tape.

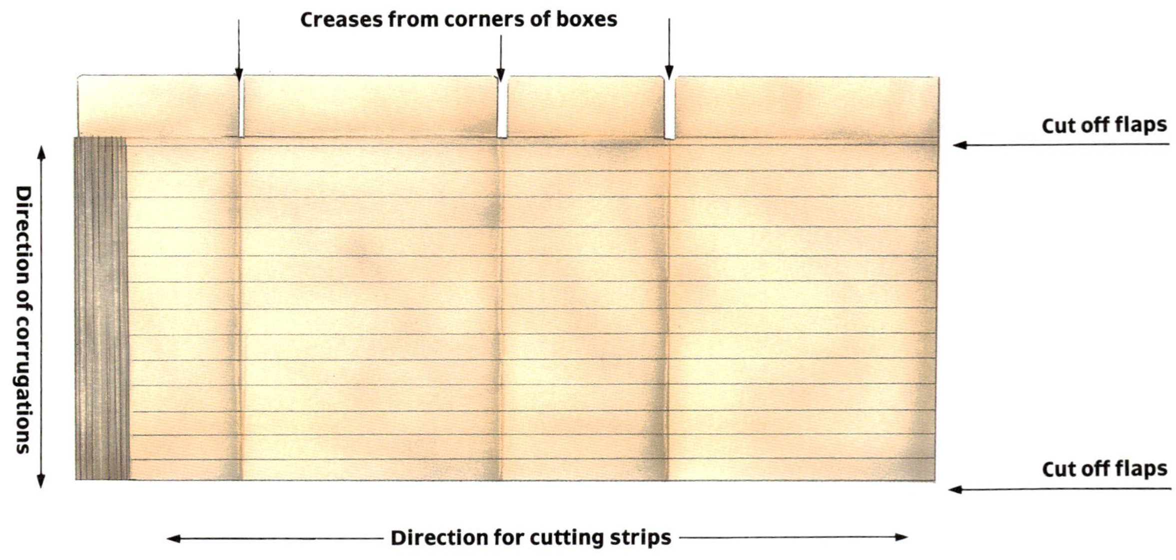

Weaving a Square Base

The number of strips used will depend on the size of basket you are making, the width of the strips, and whether it is to be square or rectangular, so the numbers of strips given here are just an example.

1

1 To make a basket with a base which has 6 strips in each direction, take 4 strips of the required length and mark the center of each. Form a cross with 2 strips in each direction and line up the marks. Weave them so that each strip goes over 1 strip and under the next.

2

2 Make sure the strips are pushed tightly together, and mark the center with an "X." Now tightly fold back one strip – **a** – which lies underneath another strip – **y**.

3
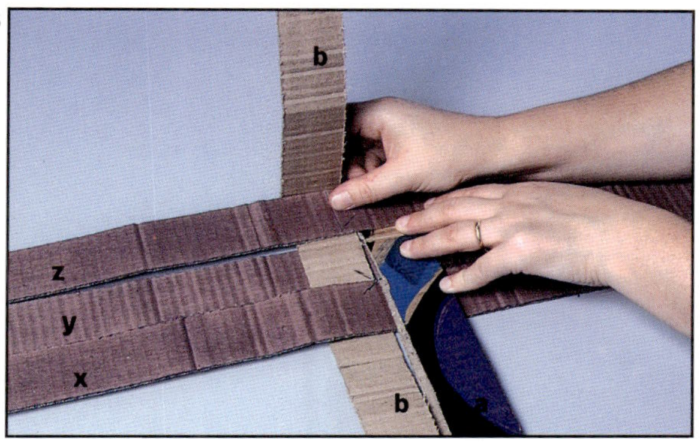

3 Place a new strip – **z** – on top of the strip still lying flat – **b**. This must be close up against the edge of the adjacent strip **y**. Then fold back strip **b** over strip **z**.

4

4 Fold strip **a** back down over **z**. Think of this side you have just been working on as **side one** of the base.

5

5 Next, working on **side two**, tightly fold back strip **y**, which lies underneath strip **b**.

6
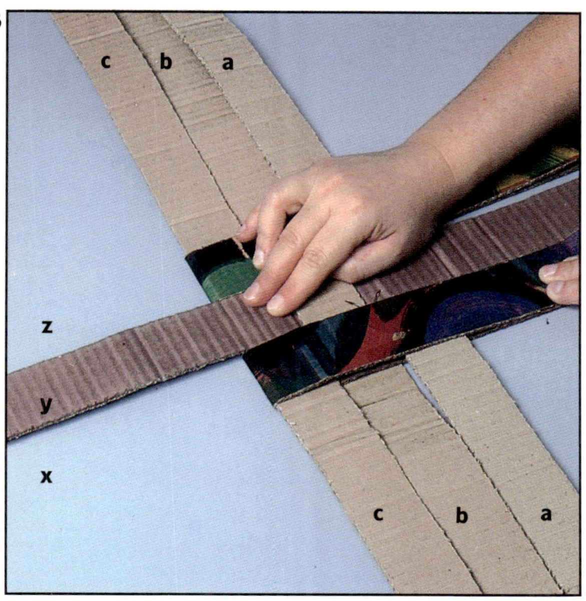

6 Lay a new strip – **c** – over strips **x** and **z**, close up to the edge of adjacent strip **b**. Fold strip **y** back down. There are now 3 strips in each direction. Add one strip each to **side three and four** to give 4 strips in each direction. Always make sure to fold tightly the relevant strips up and down when working as this keeps the weaving tight. Pin to keep the weaving tight. Check that "X" is still in the center.

7 Add another strip to each side to give 6 strips in each direction. Tighten up the weaving. The base should be flat and square with no gaps between the strips. All strips must travel over one, under one. Pin each corner.

7

Starting the Sides of a Basket

Note that the strips used for weaving the base will now be called the "spokes" and those for the sides "weavers."

1

1 Bend the spokes up. Place the end of a new strip between the 2 central spokes of one side, checking that the over 1, under 1 pattern is continued from the base up the sides. Fold the spoke from the inside tightly down over the weaver to the outside and pin. Fold the stake tightly down over the weaver to the inside and pin.

2

2 Continue this folding and pinning procedure around all 4 sides of the basket. Be careful to maintain the inside and outside folding sequence around the corners, and pin the strips which fold to the outside. At the end of each row, overlap the ends of the weaver across 3 to 4 spokes (see the photo in step 3).

3

3 Begin the second row on another side. Place the weaver between 2 central spokes so that the 2nd weaver will work the opposite to the 1st weaver, maintaining the over 1, under 1 pattern. Pin the strips which fold to the outside. Overlap ends as before.

4 Work the required number of rows, beginning each row on a different side from the previous one. Maintain the over 1, under 1 pattern and keep the tension tight so there are no gaps in the weaving.

Stitching

1 Measure a length of thread which goes around the circumference of the basket easily, with a bit extra, and double it. Thread the needle so that you are using a double thickness of thread. Make a big knot about 2½ inches from the end of the thread.

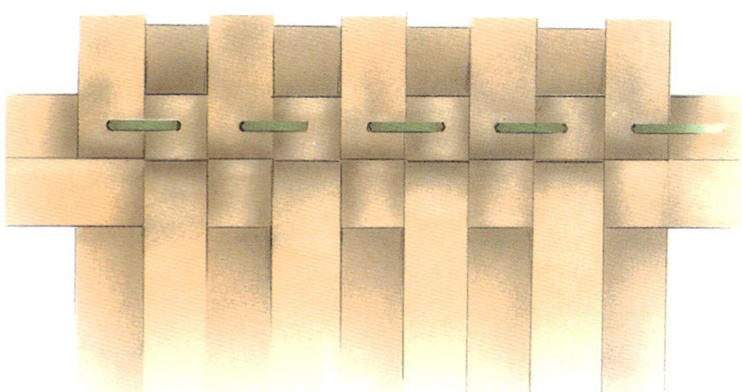

2 Start with the knot on the outside and sew around the top row of the basket, using running stitch. Keep the stitching tight and at the end of the row, tie the ends very securely. N.B.: Make sure the ends of the spokes remain upright while sewing.

Trimming the Ends of the Spokes and Weavers

1

1 When trimming the ends of the spokes, take care to cut them level with (or even fractionally below) the top edge of the last weaver.

2

2 Trim the ends of the weavers left on the outside by pulling gently on the ends and carefully cutting as close to the edge of the spoke as possible. The end of the weaver should then disappear behind the spoke. Do the same on the inside.

Joining Cardboard Strips

1

2

1 Peel away the unpainted layer and the corrugations, leaving only the top painted layer of paper to produce a flap about 2 inches long.

2 Glue the underside of the flap and stick it to the painted side of another strip. Use clothes-pins to keep it in place until it is dry. If necessary, "bandage" the seam with clear tape.

Blanket Stitch

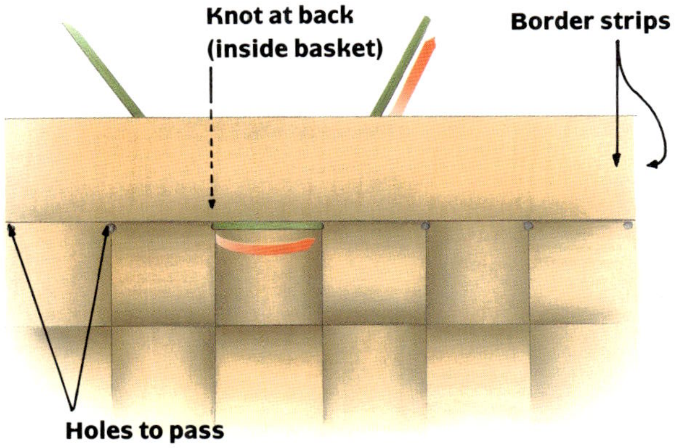

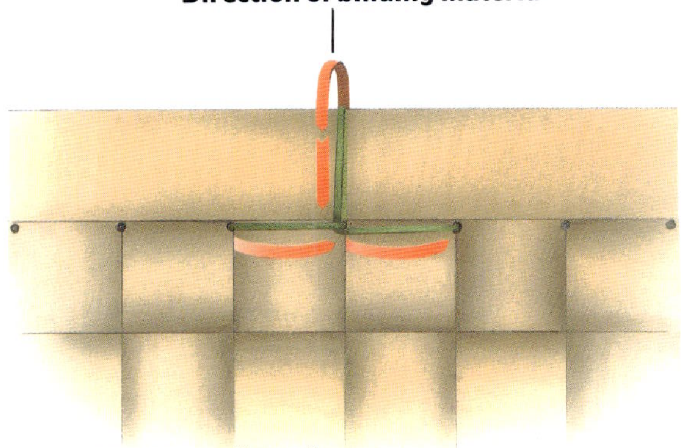

1 Measure a length of binding material about 3½ times the circumference of the basket and tie a loose knot about 6 inches from the end. Thread it through a hole (*not* at a corner) from back to front so the knot is on the inside with the long length on the outside. Thread the binding material through the next hole along, from front to back, to form a horizontal stitch.

2 Next, bring the binding material up behind the border strips, over the top of the border and thread the end down, underneath the horizontal stitch. Tighten, and check that the vertical line of the stitch is lined up with the vertical lines of the edges of the weaving stakes. Thread the end through the next hole along, and so on.

3 Work the last stitch to match the rest of the pattern – both ends should finish at the back. Undo the first knot, then tie both ends together securely under the border strips and trim the ends to about 1 inch.

"Sandwich and Sew" Border

1 Cover the back of one strip with glue and, starting on the inside of the basket, on a different side from where the last row begins and ends and not at a corner. Stick the strip to the inside of the top row. Keep this strip level with the top of the basket, and make a sharp crease around the corners. Pin to secure. Join the strips neatly using the technique for *joining strips*. Then, beginning on another side, glue a second strip to the outside of the top row.

2 Using an awl, make holes at the top corners of each of the "squares" of the row just below the border strips. The border strips are now securely bound onto the basket using blanket stitch.

Varnishing

Give the finished basket a thin coat of varnish inside and out, brushing well into the edges of the strips. Make sure there are no drips or runs. Always do your varnishing in a well-ventilated area and clean your brushes thoroughly after use.

Wastepaper Basket

This basket is made from recycled cardboard boxes. The boxes have been painted with a bold, colorful pattern, but you may prefer to choose colors that coordinate with a room in your home or workplace. It can be a good way in which to use up paint left over from decorating.

1

1 *Prepare* and paint the cardboard boxes.

You will need

- ◊ 2 to 3 large cardboard boxes
- ◊ Household vinyl paint
- ◊ Paintbrushes
- ◊ Yardstick
- ◊ Pencil
- ◊ Scissors
- ◊ Good-quality clear tape
- ◊ At least 12 spring-type clothespins
- ◊ Strong thread
- ◊ Sharp needle with large eye
- ◊ Glue stick
- ◊ Awl or skewer
- ◊ Bright-colored nylon string
- ◊ Satin finish polyurethane or acrylic varnish
- ◊ Paintbrush
- ◊ Turpentine

Techniques used

- ☞ Preparing Cardboard Strips for Weaving
- ☞ Weaving a Square Base
- ☞ Starting the Sides of a Basket
- ☞ Trimming the Ends of Spokes and Weavers
- ☞ Joining Cardboard Strips
- ☞ Stitching
- ☞ Sandwich and Sew Border
- ☞ Blanket Stitch
- ☞ Varnishing

See pages 30 to 33

2

2 Mark 24 1½-inch-wide strips 47¼ inches long on the wrong side of the prepared cardboard (this gives you 3 spare strips). Remember to cut *across* the corrugations and not along them.

3

3 Weave the base of the basket following the instructions for *weaving a square base*. When you have 6 strips in each direction, pin the corners. Then begin *weaving the sides of the basket*, as described on page 32.

4

4 Work 7 rows, beginning each row on a different side from the previous one. Maintain the over 1, under 1 pattern and keep the tension tight so there are no gaps between the weaving. Pin to secure.

5

5 Using doubled strong thread, work running *stitch* along the top row to secure the weaving. The spokes should be upright at this point. *Trim the ends* of the spokes and weavers.

6

6 Work a *sandwich and sew border*, but don't begin or end it where you began and ended the last row of the side weaving.

7

7 Glue one border strip to the inside of the top row, and, starting on another side again, glue the 2nd border strip to the outside of the top row. Overlap the ends of each strip using the technique for *joining cardboard strips*. Pin in place.

8

8 Make holes through which the binding material can pass.

9

9 Measure a length of binding material (nylon string) 3½ times the circumference of the basket. Bind the border using *blanket stitch*. *Varnish* the basket inside and out.

Shopping Basket

The method used here is similar to that used for the Wastepaper Basket, except that the Shopping Basket is rectangular instead of square.

You will need

◊ 2 to 3 large cardboard boxes
◊ Household vinyl paint (in red, yellow, green, mid-blue, and dark blue)
◊ Paintbrushes
◊ Yardstick
◊ Pencil
◊ Scissors
◊ Good-quality clear tape
◊ At least 20 spring-type clothespins
◊ Strong thread
◊ Sharp needle with large eye
◊ Glue stick
◊ Awl or skewer
◊ Colored nylon string
◊ Hole-making tool that will make large holes
◊ 4 ⅜-inch brass eyelets and punch and die kit
◊ Hammer
◊ 1 ½ yards of ⅜ inch-diameter rope
◊ Satin finish polyurethane or acrylic varnish
◊ Paintbrush
◊ Turpentine

Techniques used

☞ Preparing Cardboard Strips for Weaving
☞ Starting the Sides of a Basket
☞ Joining Cardboard Strips
☞ Trimming the Ends of Spokes and Weavers
☞ Stitching
☞ Sandwich and Sew Border
☞ Blanket Stitch
☞ Varnishing

See pages 30 to 33

1

1 *Prepare* the cardboard boxes, then paint in different colors – red, yellow, green, mid-blue, and dark blue. Leave to dry.

2 On the unpainted side of the prepared cardboard, mark and cut out 1 ½-inch-wide strips of the following lengths:

2

3 strips 43 ¼ inches long – 1 x mid-blue, 1 x dark blue, 1 x green
9 strips 31 ½ inches long – 3 x dark blue, 4 x green, 2 x mid-blue
8 strips 47 ¼ inches long – 4 x red, 3 x yellow, 1 x dark blue
(plus 2 extra in case any strips break)
Remember to cut *across* the corrugations, not along them.

3

3 Mark the center on the three 43 ¼-inch strips and lay them side by side, crossways (mid-blue/dark blue/green). Take one of the 31 ½-inch strips (dark blue) and weave it through the 3 crossways strips at the marked center points, going over the first, under the second, over the third. Mark the center point.

4

4 Weave the base by working 4 of the 31 ½-inch strips to the left of the central strip (green, mid-blue, green, dark blue). Make sure all strips travel over 1, under 1.

5

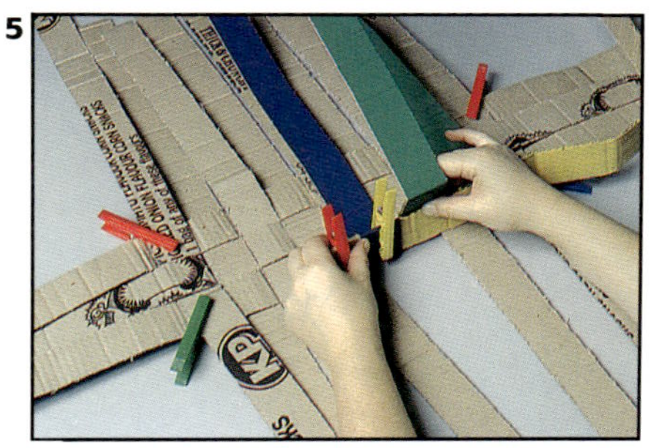

5 Repeat this last step to the right of the central strip – keep colors in the same order as step 4 – and pin the corners. You should now have a rectangle of weaving three 43 ¼-inch strips by nine 31 ½-inch strips, with the marked strip in the center. All the strips should have traveled over 1, under 1.

6

6 Take a yellow strip, and starting at a central point on a *long* edge begin *weaving the sides of the basket* using the 47 ¼-inch strips. At the end of the row, overlap the ends of the weaver across 3–4 spokes.

7

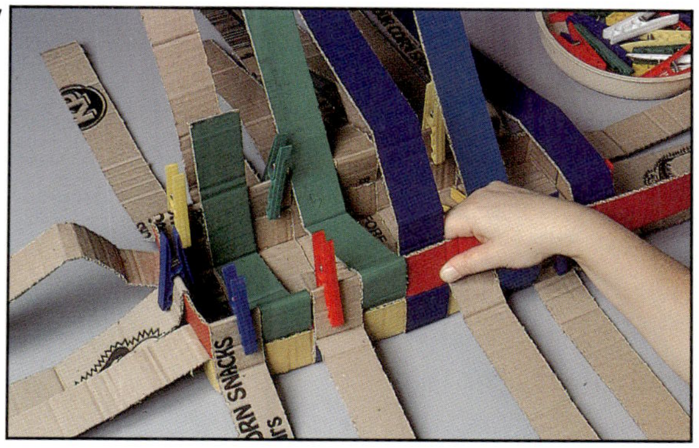

7 Using a red strip, begin the second row on the opposite long side.

8

8 Work 4 rows in this way, beginning each row on an opposite side to the one just worked (but always on a long side) and alternating the red and yellow strips. *Stitch* along the top row to secure the weaving. *Trim the ends* of the spokes and the weavers.

9

9 Begin a *sandwich and sew* border by gluing one of the dark blue 47 1/4-inch border strips to the inside of the top row of the basket and the other red one to the outside and pin in place, *joining* the ends neatly. Leave to dry.

10

10 Make holes for the binding material to pass through. Measure a length of binding material 3 1/2 times the circumference of the basket. Work *blanket stitch* to bind the border strips.

11

11 Using the hole-making tool or a large bodkin, make 2 clean holes that the brass eyelets will easily fit into on each side of the basket. These should be in the first row below the border strip, in the third "square" in from each corner, leaving 3 squares between each hole.

12

12 Insert and fix the eyelets into each hole following the manufacturer's instructions.

13

13 *Varnish* the basket inside and outside. Cut the rope for the handles in half and, if necessary, tape the ends to keep them from fraying. Pass them through the eyelets to the inside of the basket and tie knots in each end.

Square Basket with Lid

You could easily imagine Aladdin hiding his lamp in this basket, but more probably his jewels and other precious things. This is a basket in which to keep love letters, necklaces, marbles, and other special things; to stow them away out of sight and yet within easy access when the impulse to see them strikes.

You will need
- ◊ 2 to 3 large cardboard boxes
- ◊ Wax crayons
- ◊ Household vinyl paint, thinned with water
- ◊ Paintbrush
- ◊ Yardstick
- ◊ Pencil
- ◊ Scissors
- ◊ Good-quality clear tape
- ◊ At least 20 spring-type clothespins
- ◊ Strong thread
- ◊ Sharp needle with large eye
- ◊ Glue stick
- ◊ Awl or skewer
- ◊ Nylon string
- ◊ Strong quick-drying glue
- ◊ Satin finish polyurethane or acrylic varnish
- ◊ Paintbrush
- ◊ Turpentine

Techniques used
- ☞ Preparing Cardboard Strips for Weaving
- ☞ Joining Cardboard Strips
- ☞ Weaving a Square Base
- ☞ Starting the Sides of a Basket
- ☞ Trimming the Ends of the Spokes and Weavers
- ☞ Stitching
- ☞ Sandwich and Sew Border
- ☞ Blanket Stitch
- ☞ Varnishing

See pages 30 to 33

1

1 *Prepare* the cardboard boxes, then draw a random pattern over the plain side with the wax crayons and paint over the top with the thinned paint. Leave to dry.

2
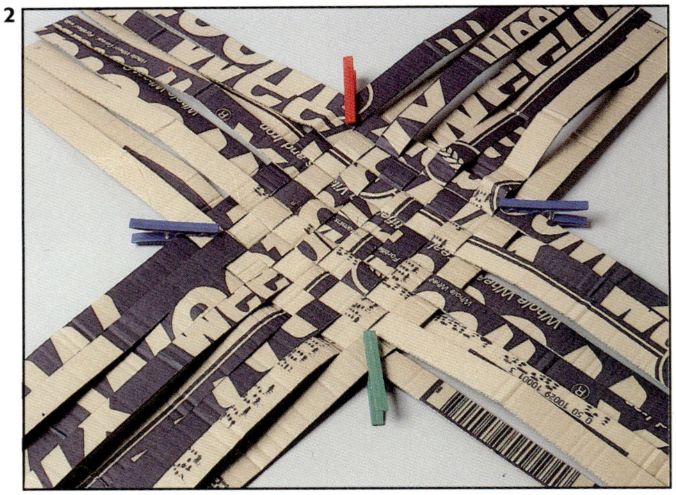

2 On the unpainted side of the cardboard, mark and cut strips 1 1/4 inches wide to give the following lengths:

For the basket
8 strips 43 1/4 inches long (for the weavers and 2 border strips)
16 strips 31 1/2 inches long (for the spokes)

For the lid
20 strips 12 inches long (for the weaving and border strips)
PLUS:
1 very long strip 118 inches long by 5/8 inches wide which will be used to form a ledge for the lid to sit on
A square of painted cardboard 12 x 12 inches

Remember to cut the strips across the corrugations, not along them. *Weave a base* 8 strips by 8 strips using the 16 31 1/2-inch strips.

3
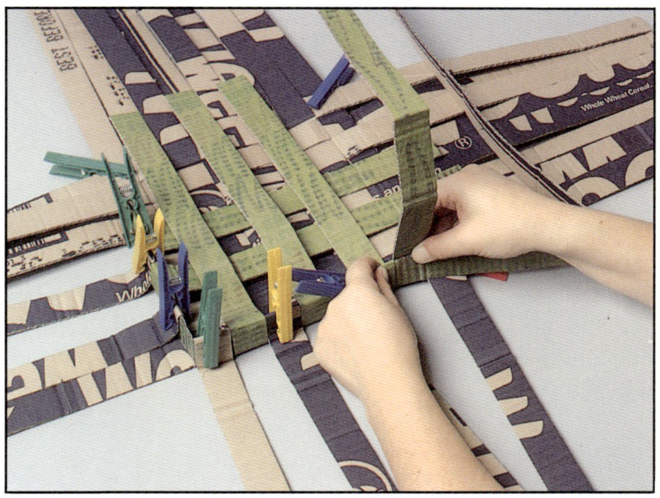

3 Begin *weaving the sides of the basket* at the center of one edge of the base, using the 43 1/4-inch strips. Begin the second row of weaving on a different side.

4

4 Weave a total of 6 rows beginning each on a different side. *Stitch* along the top row with strong thread to secure the weaving, then *trim the ends* of the spokes and the weavers.

5

5 Using the 2 remaining $43\frac{1}{4}$-inch strips, work the first stage of a *sandwich and sew border*.

6

6 Measure a length of binding material $3\frac{1}{2}$ times the circumference of the basket. Make holes under the border for this to pass through. Bind the border using *blanket stitch*.

7

7 Using the strong, quick-drying glue, stick the very long, narrow strip to the inner border strip, positioning it so that the bottom edge is level with the bottom edge of the border strip. The strip should go around the box 3 times to form a ledge 3 layers – about $\frac{3}{8}$-inch – thick.

8

8 Working with the 12-inch-long strips, weave the lid 8 strips by 8 strips in the same way as the base of the basket. Using strong thread, stitch along the last rows of weaving, working slightly toward the inside edge of this row, to secure the weaving. *Trim the ends* of the strips to leave a neat square of weaving.

9

9 Place the lid on the box and, very carefully, mark and trim the edges so that the lid will drop neatly into the basket and rest on the ledge. Make marks on the underside of the lid and on the corresponding inner side of the basket, so that you know which way around it fits best at a later stage.

10

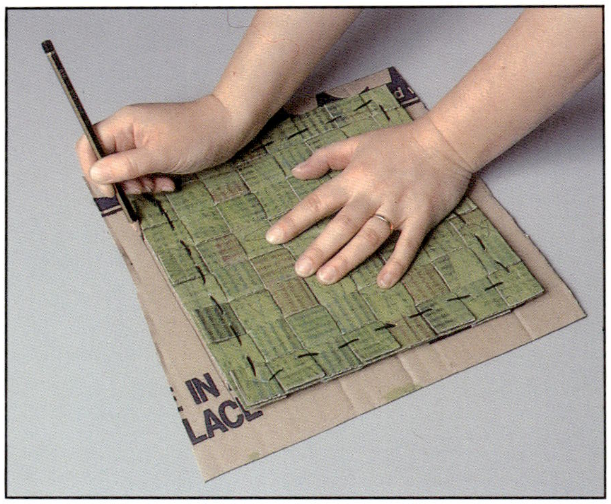

10 Lay the lid, painted side up, on the unpainted side of the cardboard square and draw around the lid and cut out the square. Mark the unpainted side of the cardboard square to correspond with the marks on the lid and inside of the box.

11

11 Glue the unpainted side of the lid and the unpainted side of the cardboard square together, matching the marked sides and the edges. Pin the two pieces together. Mark the lid again to correspond with the mark on the inner side of the basket. Weight the lid down and leave to dry overnight.

12

12 Begin a *sandwich and sew* border by gluing the 4 remaining strips along the outer edges of the painted side of the lid, lining up the inner edge of the strips with the inner edge of the last weaver. Overlap the strips at the corners (as for *joining*) to avoid bulk. Pin in place, leave to dry, then trim off the excess, following the line of the edge of the lid.

13

13 Measure a length of binding material 3½ times the circumference and bind the border strips to the lid using *blanket stitch.*

14 Using an awl, pierce a hole through the center of the lid. Thread through a loop of the binding material and knot it underneath to make a handle. *Varnish* the basket and lid inside and out.

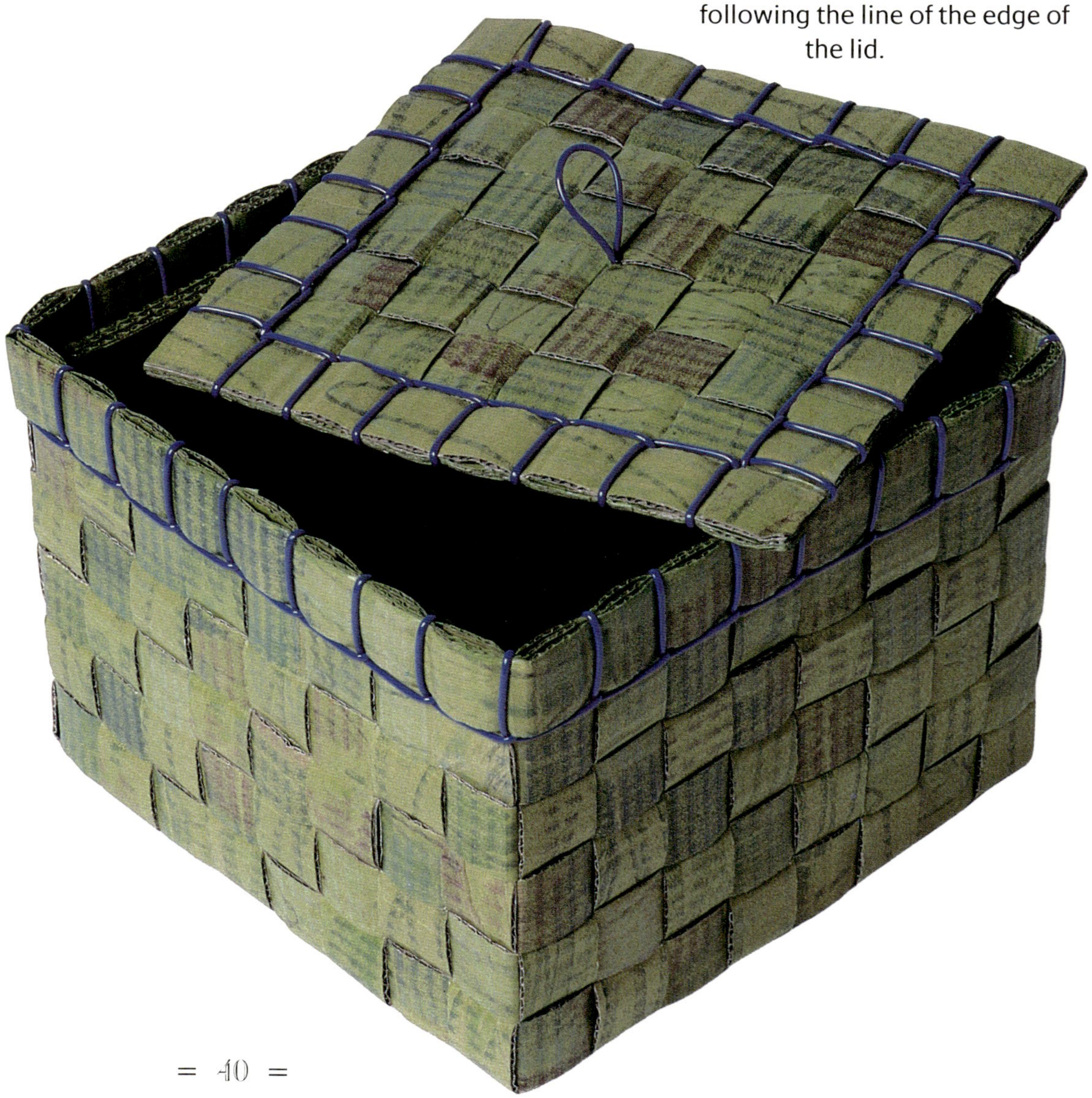

CHAPTER 3

USING RAFFIA

INTRODUCTION

Natural, as opposed to synthetic, raffia comes in two qualities: unprepared and prepared. Unprepared raffia comes in hanks of varying sizes and is sold by the pound or the half-pound. As the name suggests, the hank is a mixed bundle of raffia with strands of varying lengths, thicknesses, and quality, but hanks are ideal for making the core bundle of coiled basketry projects.

For the stitching and wrapping, use prepared raffia, which is the same material as unprepared raffia, except that the material has been selected to give more regular strands and comes in smaller bundles of 1½oz.

Natural, unprepared raffia has a neutral, creamy color, similar to cane. Raffia takes dye well, and prepared raffia can be bought already dyed.

THE TECHNIQUES YOU NEED TO KNOW TO MAKE THE PROJECTS

The projects in this chapter have certain techniques in common, and they are explained below. In the projects, the techniques used are listed below the materials and references to them in the step-by-step instructions are printed in italics. Until you are familiar with these techniques, it is best to read through the relevant sections below before starting the project. You will find useful tips and clear explanations of the techniques here that will help you achieve good results and, to avoid repetition, these are not described in detail in the projects.

Making the Core

Extract 10 or 12 strands of natural, unprepared raffia from a hank.

The Stitching Material

Select a good strand from a bundle of prepared raffia. Any strands that are too frayed and ragged to use as stitching material can be used for core material. Thread the stitching material through a needle.

Beginning a Round Base

1

1 Holding the core material in the middle, tie it in a single knot around your little finger. Take your finger out of the knot – this small loop will form the center of the base. See Diagram A.

2

2 With the knot at the top, bring all the ends of the core to the left-hand side of the loop. Hold one end of the stitching material tightly in with the core bundle. Working counterclockwise, wrap the stitching material around the loop, working down into the hole in the middle. This is important for when you begin stitching.

3

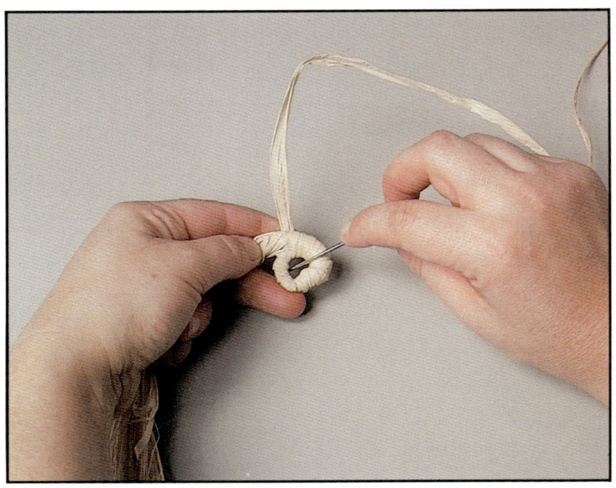

3 When you reach the knot, continue wrapping around the loop for a second round, but this time incorporate the core.

Diagram A

4

4 When you reach the knot again, instead of taking the needle down through the middle of the loop, begin to stitch by taking the needle down through the coil (row), below. Imagine that each stitch is catching 6–8 strands of the core from the row below. Work the stitches quite close together so that you cover the core. Note that the side facing you, into which you stitch down, is the right side.

Joining in New Stitching Material

With the wrong side of the mat facing, thread the new strand under the previous stitching for about ½ inch (about 4 to 5 stitches), leaving an end of about ¾ inch long sticking out. Turn the mat over so the right side is up and continue stitching with the new strand as before, incorporating the remaining length of the old stitching material into the core. When working with several colors, you can carry the different-colored strands, threaded onto a needle, in with the core bundle, picking up and dropping each color as the design specifies.

Joining in New Core Material

When the core begins to feel a bit thin, simply push more strands into the existing core until it feels the same thickness as before. This is done by folding, say, 4 strands in half, then pushing the folded ends into the center of the core and continuing to stitch as before.

Coiled Mat

Baskets made in a similar way to this mat can be found in many countries around the world and have existed in more or less this form for many hundreds of years. The swirling pattern on this mat is loosely based on that of some coiled baskets from Botswana. You can use this mat to protect surfaces from hot dishes; make half a dozen and use them as placemats, or hang a single mat on the wall as a decoration.

You will need

◊ The following amounts and types of raffia:

small hank natural, dry unprepared raffia, (about ½ pound is plenty)
1 to 2 bundles undyed prepared raffia
1 to 2 bundles black prepared raffia
1 to 2 bundles brown prepared raffia

◊ 3 sharp needles with large eyes
◊ Scissors

Techniques used

☞ Making the Core
☞ The Stitching Material
☞ Beginning a Round Base
☞ Joining in New Stitching Material
☞ Joining in New Core Material

See pages 41 to 42

1

1 Extract 10–12 strands from the natural, unprepared raffia to *make the core*. Select a good strand from a bundle of the undyed prepared raffia for the *stitching material* and *begin working a round base.*

2

2 When you have worked about 2 rows of stitching, thread a second needle with a strand of the black raffia and *join it* in, remembering to incorporate the remaining length of the undyed stitching material into the core, with the needle left on the end. Stitch around the mat until you are about a third of the way around. By now, the core will be getting a bit thin, so you will need to *join in some more core material* – do this earlier, if necessary.

3

3 With the wrong side facing, join in a strand of brown raffia, and continue stitching, carrying the black and natural stitching material in with the core, and work another third around the mat. The brown and black strands should now feel secure, so *trim the ends* left on the wrong side.

4

4 Pick up the strand of undyed raffia from the core (you can tell which it is because it will have the needle on the end) and, incorporating the brown and black strands into the core, continue stitching as before until you are within 4 or 5 stitches of the beginning of the black stitching. Pick up the black strand and stitch with it as before, incorporating the undyed and brown strands into the core until they are needed again.

5

5 Continue stitching around the mat this way, joining in more core and stitching material as necessary and following the chart for when to change color. As you work, keep the mat flat by holding the core forming the next row exactly where you want it to lie and use the stitching to hold it in place. Imagine that if you cut the mat in half and held it at eye level, you would be able to draw a straight line through the center of all the coils (see the diagram below). In order to make a good round mat, keep the thickness of the core bundle even.

Color chart

6

6 When you have worked 8 rows of the color pattern, begin the next color block. As you stitch, trim out strands from the core so the coil gradually becomes thinner and shorter as you stitch around, eventually reducing to nothing. Aim to complete this process within the one color block.

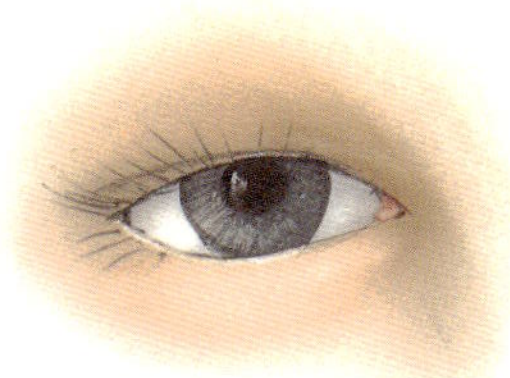

Eye level

7

7 At the end you will be stitching over only 4 or 5 strands of core. Finish the mat by threading the strand of stitching material back through the stitching for about 2 inches, and then carefully cut it off close to the stitching so it slips behind it.

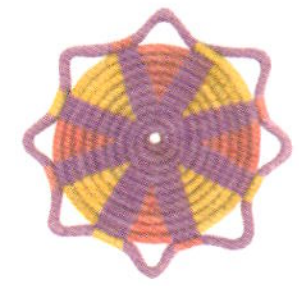

Coiled Basket

If you think that this small basket is perfect for nuts and candy, you are right! This style of basket is often found in North Africa and the Middle East – the decorative pointed border is particularly reminiscent of coiled baskets from these areas.

You will need

◊ The following amounts and types of raffia:
  small hank natural dry raffia, unprepared (about ½ pound is plenty)
  1 to 2 bundles purple prepared raffia
  1 to 2 bundles yellow prepared raffia
  1 to 2 bundles pink prepared raffia

◊ 3 sharp needles with large eyes
◊ Scissors

Techniques used

☞ Making the Core
☞ The Stitching Material
☞ Beginning a Round Base
☞ Joining in New Stitching Material
☞ Joining in New Core Material
See pages 41 to 42

Pattern chart with detail

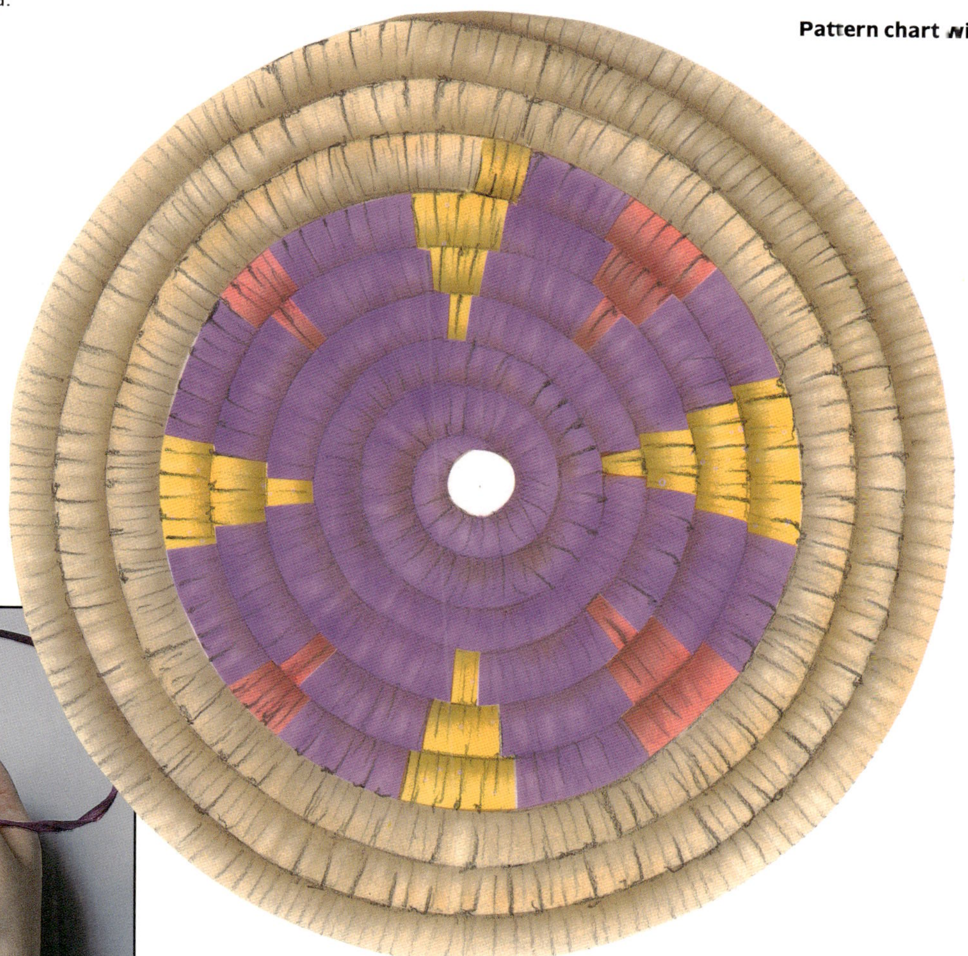

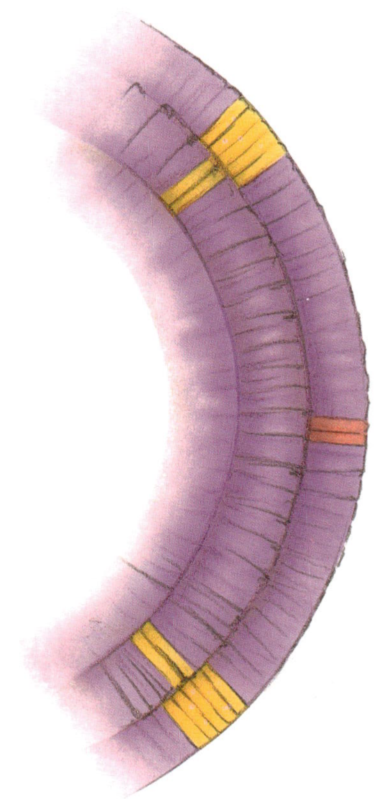

1 Extract 10–12 strands from the natural, unprepared raffia to *make the core*. Select a good strand from a bundle of the purple prepared raffia for the *stitching material* and *begin a round base*.

2 When you have worked 2 to 3 rows of stitching, start following the pattern chart above. *Join in* a strand of yellow prepared raffia and at 4 equidistant points, work 1 or 2 yellow stitches. Continue using purple for the rest of the stitching. Then join in a pink strand and, following the pattern chart, at 4 points halfway between the yellow stitches, work 1 or 2 pink stitches. On this same row, work 4–6 yellow stitches above those of the previous row (see the detail of the pattern chart). As before, the remaining stitching is purple. Join in new stitching or core material where necessary, carrying the other stitching strands in with the core bundle while they are not being used. *Trim* the ends of the joined-in strands when you feel they are secure.

3

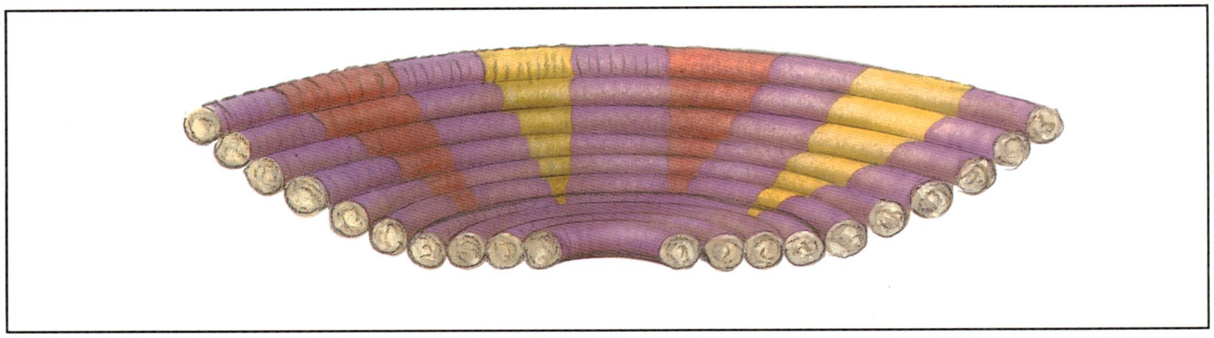

3 At the end of the third row of the pattern, begin shaping the basket by holding the bundle of core material slightly up from – rather than directly in line with – the coil of the previous row (the photograph shows how to hold the basket and core material to achieve this). Imagine you are molding the basket. The diagram above shows how the curve is formed over several rows – it is a matter of holding the core material in the correct place and using each stitch to hold it there. When you begin shaping the basket, gradually increase the thickness of the core material until it is $3/8$–$5/8$ inch in diameter when stitched.

3

4

4 Continue working round in an anticlockwise direction, following the pattern charts. You might find it helpful to thread up several needles in preparation as there are a number of colour changes involved. Control the shape all the time, looking at the basket from different angles as you work to check that it is developing as evenly as possible.

5

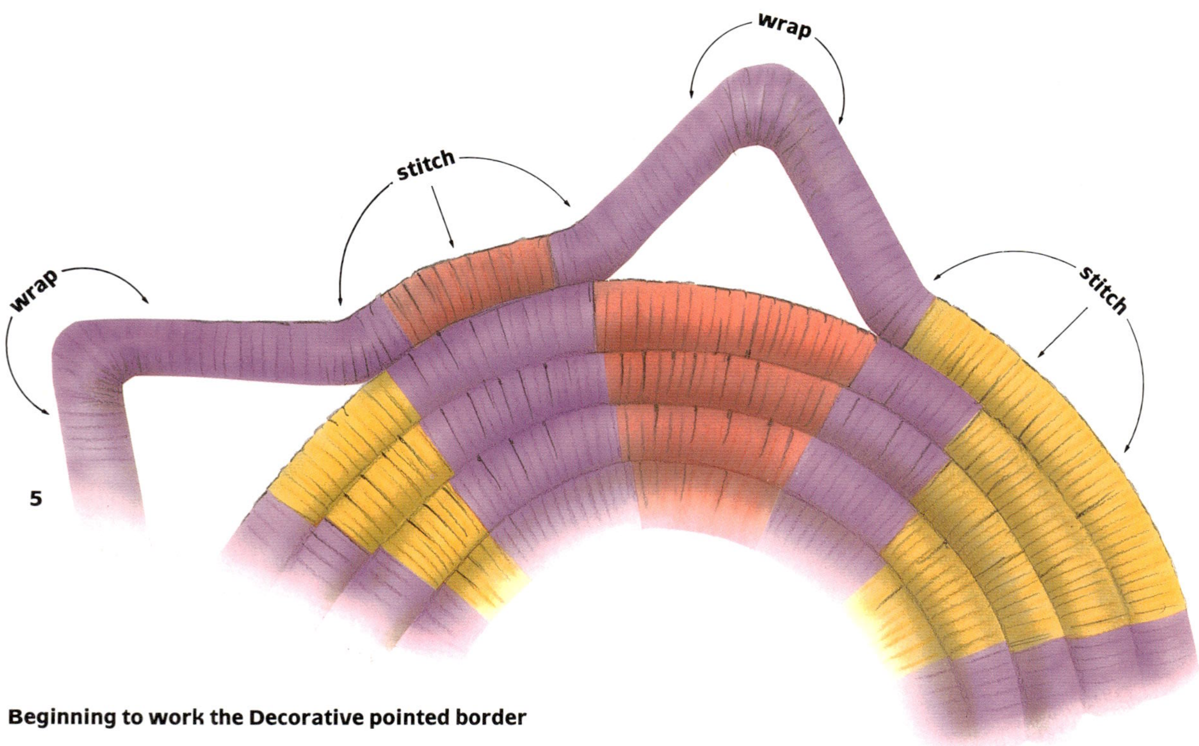

Beginning to work the Decorative pointed border

5 At the end of the seventh row of the pattern (you should finish with a yellow block of stitching), begin working the decorative pointed border. Trim a few strands out of the core to produce a slightly thinner bundle, and continue stitching in yellow until just before you reach the pink block of the previous row. Pick up the purple strand, work 3 or 4 stitches, and then wrap (not stitch) the core tightly until you have enough to form the point, bending the wrapped core into shape. Work a few stitches in purple just past the pink block, securing the point in position.

Pick up the pink strand and stitch until just before the yellow block of the previous row. Pick up the purple strand, work 2 or 3 stitches, then wrap (not stitch) the core to form a second point to match the first.

6 Secure it just past the yellow block of the previous row with 2 stitches – x.

Next pick up the yellow strand and stitch until just before the pink block. Continue this way around the basket, following the pattern in the diagram, right, until you have wrapped the eighth and last point. Secure this point with 4 or 5 stitches.

Then trim away most of the core so that when you continue stitching, it very quickly tapers away to nothing. Stitch very securely over these ends, then thread the stitching strand back through the stitching for a little way and trim the end.

6

Complete pattern and border

ACKNOWLEDGEMENTS

I would like to acknowledge the following people who have helped me either in becoming a basketmaker, or in the preparation of this book, or both: Jill Brownbill, one of my art teachers from school who encouraged me through idle teenage years and believed, I think, that I'd do something worthwhile one day.

Lois Walpole and Mary Butcher, two of my tutors at the (ex-) London College of Furniture (now London Guildhall University), both of whom taught me much of what I know about basketry. Lois's own work was not only an inspiration to me but also a revelation; Mary has opened many doors for me in terms of basketry as a subject to be explored historically and ethnographically.

Dick Speed of Technology Associates, Oxon, who put my name forward as an author for this book.

The Basketmakers' Association and the Society of Designer Craftsmen, both of which have been supportive of my basketmaking ventures.

Many friends have helped me with this book, especially Mike Kidron and Mary Butcher, by reading and commenting on the text and generally egging me on. Last, but not least, Stefanie Foster, my editor at Quintet, and Ian Howes who took the photographs.

BASKETMAKER CONTACTS AND SUPPLIERS

UK

The Secretary of the Basketmakers' Association
Ann Brooks
Pond Cottage
North Road
Chesham Bois
Bucks HP6 5NA

USA

Mr. Jim Widess
926 Gilman Street
Berkeley
CA 94710

Mrs. Judith Olney
34 Bradford Street
Rowley
MA 01969

Mrs. Linda Lugenbill
361 Silver Springs Court
Colorado Springs
CO 80919

CANADA

Ms Ankaret Dean
RRI McDonalds Corners
Ontario K0G 1M0

Mrs. Joleen Gordon
121 Crichton Avenue
Dartmouth
Nova Scotia B3A 3R6

AUSTRALIA

Mrs. Sally King
PO Box 473
Ulverstone
Tasmania 7315

Mrs. Jean Stone
Basketmakers of Victoria Inc
3 Loudon Road
Burwood
Victoria 3125

Thanks to Mrs. Linda Lugenbill for her help and advice.

FURTHER READING

Harvey, Virginia *The Techniques of Basketry* (Batsford)
Hoppe, Flo *Wicker Basketry* (Interweave Press)
La Plantz, Shereen *Plaited Basketry: The Woven Form* (Press de La Plantz)
Walpole, Lois *Creative Basketmaking* (Collins)
Wright, Dorothy *The Complete Book of Baskets and Basketry* (David & Charles)